CREATION

AND THE

FLOOD

A Journey of
Scripture, Science and Faith

JOHN K. GRIFFIN, PhD

PROCLAMATION
PUBLISHING

Published in Potomac, MD, by Proclamation Publishing Company. www.proclamationpublishing.com.

ISBN 978-1-7347292-0-7 (paperback)

ISBN 978-1-7347292-1-4 (ebook)

Acknowledgments

Projects like this don't get completed without great support. To my entire family, thank you for your patience with me for all the time I spent on this endeavor. To my wife, I appreciate your encouraging me to write about my journey and your pushing me to refine my voice. To friends who reviewed portions of the manuscript, I value your input and appreciate your time and effort.

CONTENTS

PART III The Flood

PART I

Perspectives

CHAPTER 1

···

Crisis

"Daddy, did dinosaurs exist?"

They sure did, about 65 million years ago, I was about to say, when … uh-oh. I hesitated. Instead, I told Sam, who was nine, that I would get back to him on that. *Wow. That was weird*, I thought, surprised that I didn't answer such a simple question right away. However, I could envision the conversation going places I was not prepared for, and I wanted to get my ducks in a row before having this discussion with Sam or any of my other three kids.

The problem was the age of the earth. How would I respond to Sam if he told me his teacher said that dinosaurs did not exist, or that dinosaurs and humans had lived at the same time? The kids all went to a Christian school at that time, and I was not aware of what the school was teaching with regard to the age of the earth. If I was going to contradict what the kids were learning at school, I wanted to go about it carefully and gently.

Eventually, I simply told Sam that dinosaurs "existed, a long time ago." Thankfully, he did not press me on the timeline, so I was able to leave the timing vague. I changed the subject, happy to be able to avoid a potentially thorny conversation.

Although the parenting crisis had passed—at least temporarily—

Sam's question, as children's simple and innocent questions sometimes do, revealed another problem. The Bible appeared to make some claims that I didn't think were true. I believed that dinosaurs existed 65 million years ago, yet the Bible seemed to be saying that the earth was created in a week, and very recently. This issue—my trust in the Bible—cut to the core of my relationship with my Lord. The realization that I had a big problem to solve hit me hard.

How did I get here? I was in my mid-40s, after all. Why hadn't I dealt with and resolved this before? Well, for most of my life I had attended churches that had flexible interpretations of early Genesis. I guess I had taken that as license to just not get hung up on things like six-day creation. In the previous couple of years, however, I had been worshipping at a nondenominational evangelical church. During that time my faith had really blossomed, and my relationship with Jesus had risen to a whole new level. Part and parcel of that was taking the Bible very seriously. My faith was strengthened and my life was transformed by opening my mind and heart to the truth of God's love for me, as revealed to me personally in His Holy Word. And I trust that His Word is truth; indeed I rely on it being truth.

What then was I supposed to do with early Genesis? God seemed to be telling me He created the world in six days, 6,000 years ago; I felt certain that wasn't true. God seemed to be telling me that there was a global flood, covering the top of Mount Everest, perhaps four or five thousand years ago; I was confident that wasn't true either. The Bible seemed to claim that all humanity descended from one couple; I wasn't sure what to think about evolution. In short, I had a science versus Scripture problem.

This was more than an academic, theoretical problem for me. This was a relationship issue. My relationship with my Lord is the primary relationship in my life. Why was God asking me to believe things that weren't true? Did the Bible say false things? And if early Genesis was not true, could I trust the New Testament? If I had encountered this challenge earlier in my life, my belief may not have survived. If Christ hadn't been living inside of me, my faith may have been seriously damaged. As it was, even though I had that strong anchor, I did still entertain some doubts. The outer walls of my faith were under assault and in danger of being breached. This was the biggest challenge to my faith I can remember. My relationship with God was under strain. Although I continued to pray and read the Bible, I didn't anticipate or enjoy these experiences like I used to. I felt a sadness, a distance, and trepidation.

There were also significant practical implications to my struggles. I had recently gotten remarried, and our marriage was built on our shared faith. My wife would not have married me if not for my relationship with Jesus. She depended on it. How unfair to her, who had trusted in the steadfastness of my faith, that now I was struggling! Moreover, I was the spiritual leader of my family with four kids aged seven to eleven. How well could I guide and encourage their faith formation if I was struggling? And what would we teach our kids about early Genesis? It's tough to avoid Noah's ark with young kids.

I was scared, and I needed to face my fears. I went to the Bible. I also began lots of extrabiblical reading and research, devouring books written by biblical scholars, examining websites and blogs run by Christian organizations, and so forth. And I poured more focus and energy into my prayer life.

At first, it did not go well. That's an understatement, actually. To begin my research, I wanted to buy a new study Bible, one that I hoped would offer more detailed commentary than what my old study Bible contained. I looked to the leader of a small-group Bible study I had recently attended for insight. His preparation was always impeccable, and he drew heavily on the work of John MacArthur, so I figured I would buy *The MacArthur Study Bible*. I eagerly awaited its arrival. As soon as it arrived, I opened it up and went straight to the note on Genesis 1:1 and read:

This description of God creating heaven and earth is understood to be: 1) recent, i.e., thousands not millions of years ago; 2) ex-nihilo, i.e., out of nothing; and 3) special, i.e., in six consecutive 24-hour periods called "days" and further distinguished as such by this phrase, "there was evening and there was morning." Scripture does not support a creation date earlier than about 10,000 years ago.[1]

Oh no. That was deflating. What I had hoped would help me instead made me feel worse. (This isn't a criticism of the book itself. I still often use *The MacArthur Study Bible* for my daily Scripture reading because its thorough, detailed notes otherwise have been very helpful. He has done a great deal of marvelous work over his career.)

Next, I figured I would search my church's website to see if there were any archived sermons on Genesis. Turns out there had indeed been a series on Genesis several years ago by a since-retired pastor whom I respect a lot. I pulled up the text of the first sermon in the series and started reading. He was emphatic that early Genesis is literally true in its every word. God created the earth in six 24-hour days. The flood of Noah killed all but eight people. And for good measure, he argued that the reliability of the New Testament is linked to the historicity of Genesis. Well, that wasn't helpful either. My initial research was leading me further into crisis.

The situation was a bit ironic, really. One would expect, I suppose, challenges to your faith to come from people *outside* of the church. Arguments from atheists, for example. However, it was claims from Christians that were causing my consternation. The words of this sincere, God-loving Christian pastor had helped me grow significantly in my faith—yet now his words posed a challenge to my faith!

I have a soft spot in my heart for my former pastor. He is a smart and talented preacher. He has zeal for the gospel and a tireless passion for evangelism, and he has guided countless people toward Christ.

Scores upon scores of former unbelievers have met the living God in his church. I experienced real growth in my relationship with Christ while in his church. And I have had several conversations with other members of my church wherein they have shared with me, unprompted, the positive role he has played in their faith development and Christian walk. I pray that the Lord may somehow use me some tiny fraction as much as He has used this pastor for the growth of His kingdom.

This particular message of his, however, scared me. And now I was becoming bewildered. If the Bible really taught that the earth was created in six days, less than ten thousand years ago, my trust in the Bible would be fractured. I even spoke out in frustration against God, asking Him why He was asking me to believe things that were not true.

The crisis started to turn when I found Galileo's *Letter to Christina*, which gave me a lot of comfort and encouragement.[2] Galileo wrote the letter to the grand duchess of Tuscany in an effort to convince her of the compatibility of Copernicanism and Scripture. He faced a science vs. Bible conflict in his day as to whether the sun circled the earth or the earth circled around the sun. Galileo was taking heat for his scientific view that the earth rotates on its axis and revolves around the sun, as at the time this was widely believed to contradict the Bible. Dozens of Bible verses were cited in his day in support of a stationary earth. Examples, a couple among many, include Psalm 104:5, "He set the earth on its foundations, so that it should never be moved," and Ecclesiastes 1:5, "The sun rises, and the sun goes down, and hastens to the place where it rises." Indeed, Galileo would later be condemned by the Roman Inquisition for heresy, and his heliocentric publications were banned by the church. He spent the last decade of his life under house arrest.

Galileo argued that God reveals Himself both through His Word and through His creation, and when both His Word and His creation are properly interpreted, there can be no contradiction. Sometimes, science helps us interpret Scripture. We all do this today. When we read Isaiah 11:12—"He will raise a signal for the nations and will assemble the banished of Israel, and gather the dispersed of Judah from the four corners of the earth"—we don't even pause to consider the idea of an earth with four literal corners. We don't pause to consider because we know that the science dictates that the phrase not be taken literally.

Modern science is not infallible, of course. Scientists are human, their tools may be inadequate, and the base of knowledge they work with may be incomplete. If you go back to any previous period in human history, you will see that the scientists of that day had, in many instances, reached incorrect conclusions. There is no reason to expect our current period to be different. We learn more over time, and in the process we discover that things we thought were true are actually not. Still, in many cases the evidence at hand is so compelling that it makes sense to be highly confident that what we think is true actually is true. We are right to be highly confident that the earth is not flat.

Galileo argued that when well-supported science and a literalistic interpretation of the Bible conflict, then it is likely that the literalistic interpretation of the Bible is in error. And that when the Bible is properly understood, it does not contradict science:

I think in the first place that it is very pious to say and prudent to affirm that the holy Bible can never speak untruth—whenever its true meaning is understood. But I believe nobody will deny that it is often very abstruse, and may say things which are quite different from what its bare words signify. Hence in expounding the Bible if one were always to confine oneself to the unadorned grammatical meaning, one might fall into error. Not only contradictions and propositions far from true might thus be made to appear in the Bible, but even grave heresies and follies.[3]

Galileo also argued that the Bible is more concerned with theological teaching than with science. For instance, he quoted a presumably private conversation with, tradition has it, Cardinal Baronius (1538–1607), to say "that the intention of the Holy Ghost is to teach us how one goes to heaven, not how heaven goes."

Encouraged by these arguments, I set about continuing my research and study. In the course of my work I have learned a great deal about the Bible and have grown closer to Jesus. There have certainly been periods of struggle and frustration, but I believe that God welcomes my striving to understand Him. What has helped most is trusting, with patience and humility, that the Lord would lead me safely through these thickets. The Lord has been gracious to me and patient with me regarding my doubts. He responded by inviting me to draw nearer to Him. He truly is faithful. He really did love me first, and He will never let go of me. I love Him.

With regard to creation and the flood, in the end I arrived at a place where I do not have internal conflicts between my faith and my scientific knowledge and where I do not see contradictions between science and Scripture. The whole Bible is true; the earth is old; there was no global flood. I am confident in all three of these assertions. With regard to evolution, I am still working through that issue and, God willing, will write a book about it in the future. However, due to my success in dealing with Genesis 1 and the flood, and due to the spiritual growth that I have experienced in the process, I have great faith and confidence that in the end there will be no reason to doubt the truthfulness of the Bible.

My prayer for this book is that it will give encouragement, comfort, and support to others who struggle with faith and science issues. If you are a Christian who wrestles with the literal interpretation of early Genesis, I want you to know that there are sound and responsible ways to interpret the creation and flood accounts, such that the passages do not contradict science. If you are a potential follower of Christ for whom the creation and flood accounts are a hurdle to belief, I want to encourage you to keep engaging because there are ways over that hurdle. And for anyone, Christian or non-Christian alike, who is curious about early Genesis, I want to invite you to spend time with the text in its historical and cultural context. There really is a lot of fascinating stuff to learn.

Notes

1   John MacArthur, *The MacArthur Study Bible* (Wheaton, IL: Crossway, 2010), 17.

2   Galileo Galilei, *Letter to the Grand Duchess Christina of Tuscany, 1615*. Stanford University, accessed March 19, 2020, https://web.stanford.edu/~jsabol/certainty/readings/Galileo-LetterDuchessChristina.pdf.

3   Galileo, *Letter to the Grand Duchess.*

CHAPTER 2

....

Foundations

Before diving into Genesis 1 and the flood, it may be useful for context if I provide you with a window into what I believe as a Christian and how I approach the Bible. I am a sinner, saved by grace, through faith in Jesus. I am saved only through faith, not by works or anything else. I have a personal relationship with Jesus, the living God, and strive to make that relationship the foundation of my life. I believe that every Christian, from the moment of salvation, has God, in the form of the Holy Spirit, living inside them. I believe that Jesus is the Son of God. I believe in His virgin birth and that He was both God and human. I believe that He rose from the dead, and I believe He will return to judge both the living and the dead. I trust Him and know that He cares for me and loves me deeply. When I pray, my Father hears me, and if I pray in accord with His will, He answers my prayers. I also believe that frequent reading of the Bible, reflection on God's Word, and prayer are vital to the spiritual development of a believer.

Growing up I went to church and was religious but, truly, I was lost in plain sight. At the age of 23 I gave my life to Jesus and began a relationship with Him. Two things in particular helped me. One was the writings of Augustine, especially his *Confessions*, where he talked in personal and emotional terms of his relationship with God. I was convicted and recognized that I needed, and deep down wanted, a personal relationship with Jesus. The other was a vibrant and youthful church that I attended for a time in New York City. I found the biblical teaching and the fellowship immensely helpful. But I didn't stay in New York long, moving to Philadelphia to attend business school. My growth over the rest of my twenties and into my thirties was, unfortunately, tepid: two steps forward, one step back, with long periods of stagnation as well.

During my mid-thirties and into my early forties, the Lord made use of episodes of difficulty and pain to lead me to lean on Him and to trust Him. There was an episode of cancer, a relatively large malignant melanoma tumor that was removed before it spread. Then there was the loss of an enjoyable and promising career, followed by prolonged unemployment. Most significant, however, was the illness and passing of my late wife. It was crushing to see her, whom I loved so dearly, go through such a painful experience and endure so much emotional and physical suffering. Yet I was inspired to see that she did not suffer spiritually. In fact, she was an encouragement to me in that regard. She had a vibrant prayer life, and she took the opportunity of her illness to witness to those around her. As for my own relationship with the Lord at that time, He taught me to depend upon Him and to trust Him. I acknowledged His sovereignty even when I did not understand why He chose to do what He did. And I came to depend upon Him to make it through each day, developing trust and knowledge that He cared for me. The grace I received in the presence of the Holy Spirit enabled me to do all that was required: serving as Susan's primary physical, emotional, and spiritual caregiver; dealing with the pain and loss and disappointment of seeing a loved one suffer and die; shepherding our two children through the ordeal; and carrying on a full-time job. I was powerless yet strong in my weakness as I depended upon my Lord.[4]

Shortly after Susan's passing, I moved to an evangelical church. I found the teaching to be biblically based and theologically sound, with the power to cultivate growth. Becoming integrated into the church community—getting to know Christian brothers and sisters and seeing them walk and grow in their relationship with the Lord—was an encouragement to me in my own walk. Finding fruitful ministry opportunities led to more spiritual maturity. My desire to spend time with the Lord grew. My prayer life deepened, and I enjoyed the experience of reading Scripture daily. All this strengthened my relationship with God. More recently, writing this book led to another step forward in my relationship with God. There were plenty of times of discomfort as I struggled and wrestled with Scripture, but my faith is now stronger for having gone through it. The key was trusting that God would see me through safely.

And I have seen fruit in my life, even just in the past couple of years. I get angry less often, and when I do get angry, I am better able to bridle my tongue. I used to curse and use coarse humor, but those behaviors are gone now. I find myself to be less prideful, less impatient, and less concerned with material possessions. Fewer things make me anxious, though I still battle anxiety periodically.[5] My time is spent less in worldly culture and more in Scripture and worship. I am starting, slowly, to encourage others in their faith journeys by being more open about my own faith; I also reach out to others by leading a Bible study and serving in a ministry where I provide one-on-one caregiving. Now, as my family could tell you, I struggle with sin and I fail. Thank God for His grace! I have nothing to boast about, except that the Spirit is guiding me in the right direction. I follow, albeit slower than I should, because I want a closer relationship with Jesus and I love Him.

As for how I approach the Bible, the following is a set of broad considerations that are relevant to the analysis in this book. Some of these perspectives I brought with me into this endeavor, and some I developed over the course of my research and learning.

I trust that the Bible is true in all that it intends to teach—that the Bible is God's Word, spoken through human authors, and that the authors were inspired by the Holy Spirit. This is ultimately a matter of faith. I believe that God gave us the Bible so that He could reveal

Himself to us, and that He therefore gave us a Bible that is free from error in its teachings. He achieved this through miracles of the Holy Spirit, both inspiring the human authors and, later, directing which books made it into the Bible.

The assertion that the Bible is truth does not mean that it always needs to be taken literally, but rather interpreted responsibly. When Jesus says in John 10:9, "I am the door," He does not mean that He is made of wood. He is speaking figuratively, declaring that He is the entryway to salvation. Figurative language is plentiful in the Bible, but these passages are no less true. Indeed, figurative language is good for isolating and highlighting truth and is often employed for that purpose in Scripture. Examples of figurative devices in the Bible include metaphor, simile, imagery, personification, hyperbole, apostrophe, anthropomorphism, irony, sarcasm, idiom, euphemism, and more. The Bible truly is sophisticated writing.

How do we determine whether to interpret a passage literally or figuratively? It helps to begin by trying to assess the type of writing—the genre of the passage—as that will guide us as to what to expect from the text. The Bible has many genres: narrative, poetry, genealogy, parables, history, apocalyptic literature, saga, and more. It is important to understand the genre of a passage in order to properly interpret it. Narrative should be interpreted differently than, say, poetry. For example, Luke 24:2–3 is clearly literal: "And they found the stone rolled away from the tomb, but when they went in they did not find the body of the Lord Jesus." This is a factual narrative. On the other hand, Song of Solomon 4:1 is clearly figurative: "Your hair is like a flock of goats leaping down the slopes of Gilead." This is a love poem. Sometimes, unlike the examples I just gave, it is hard to discern the genre. The first eleven chapters of Genesis provide a notable example.

Once the genre has been determined, it is critical to assess the context of the passage, perhaps especially with respect to the surrounding text, but also with respect to the book and even the Bible as a whole. Imbedded in contextual analysis is a consideration of the time, place, and culture of the author and audience. Finally, a keen inspection of the exact wording is needed. Any knowledge of the original language can be quite helpful. What do we do when still in doubt as to whether to interpret a passage literally or figuratively? One approach is simple trial and error: begin with a literal interpretation, and if that doesn't fit, try a figurative approach.

One important point deserves emphasis here. When considering the context of a passage, it is vital to understand the culture and setting. This is because while Scripture was written for us, it was not written to us. The Old Testament was written to Israel, and the New Testament was written to first-century audiences. The Bible is an ancient document, written in languages that most of us do not understand, with its primary audiences very far removed from us in terms of culture and geography. In order to properly understand a passage, we need to try to understand how the original audience would have understood it in their historical and cultural context. The quote above from Song of Solomon is a great example: "Your hair is like a flock of goats leaping down the slopes of Gilead." Reading those words with modern urban or suburban American lenses, we do not necessarily view the comparison as a compliment! As well, the import of the author's reference to Gilead is likely lost on us.

Another key thing I learned in my study is that sometimes the Lord "accommodates" to the audience. The Lord explains things to them in terms of their current understanding—which was scientifically basic. For example, in 600 BC people believed that the sun literally rose and fell over a flat earth and that the sky, including what we now call space, was confined directly beneath the sun. And so we get Psalm 19:6, which says of the sun, "Its rising is from the end of the heavens, and its circuit to the end of them."

We also get the parable of the mustard seed, which Jesus calls in Mark 4:31 "the smallest of all the seeds on earth." It is not, but it was the smallest seed that the Israelites knew about. Jesus accommodated to the hearers' scientific knowledge in order to make a theological point: His kingdom, from a small beginning, would grow and spread throughout the world. Purpose and context are important when recognizing the proper role for accommodation. Here, Jesus was not trying to teach the Israelites a biology or botany lesson. He was teaching about His kingdom and using science to do so. The truth that is taught here is about the kingdom of God, not about the physical dimensions of the mustard seed in relation to other seeds.

Finally, hearkening back to Galileo, I wish to emphasize that God has revealed Himself both through His Word and through the physical world. The Bible and the book of nature will not be in contradiction when both are properly understood. If there is a seeming contradiction, then our interpretation of one or the other or both must be in error. Importantly, much as we already do with issues such as whether the earth revolves around the sun, we can use the book of nature to point out to us other areas where we may not be employing the best scriptural interpretation. Such as six-day creation.

Notes

4   One way in which He supported me was sending help in the form of family and friends, to whom I am exceedingly grateful.

5   I want to stress that in many cases anxiety is not a sign of a lack of faith. It can be related to personality type and brain chemistry, among other things. And we are all human and prone to worry. My point is that, in many instances, walking with God can bring peace.

PART II

Creation

CHAPTER 3

··

Teaching a Young Earth

The teachings of John MacArthur and of the retired pastor of my church are commonplace in American Protestantism. A 2013 poll conducted by Biologos reveals that a slight majority of pastors self-identified as young earth creationists (YECs), and that "non-Mainline, Charismatic, and Southern Baptist pastors were overwhelmingly Young Earth Creationists."[6] YECs are numerous and influential in the Christian community. Prominent organizations include Answers in Genesis and Creation Ministries International, both of which teach that creation took place in six 24-hour days about 6,000 years ago. Young earth creationism appears to be the dominant viewpoint in conservative American churches.

A literal, concrete reading of Genesis, wherein the Bible teaches that the earth was created in six 24-hour days roughly 6,000 years ago, is the most straightforward way to approach the text. Whether it is the best way is debatable. Sometimes, literal interpretations are best. Sometimes they are not. For me, the literal interpretation of the creation account is not a viable position. In my view, the scientific evidence against it is just too compelling. Others may differ with me on the extent to which we should use science to assess the Bible, or they may interpret the science itself differently. But the most compelling evidence I've seen shows that the earth is old, and I read the Bible in light of that knowledge. Being asked to stick to a concrete reading of Genesis 1, then, was a big challenge for me.

The problem was that I didn't have another way to look at the text. As I'll explain, I tried to read the "days" as being very long periods of time, but in the end I couldn't subscribe to that rendering. And so I became worried that the Bible teaches something that isn't true. Eventually, guided by lots of great commentators and scholars, I was able to dig below the surface of the text. By learning how the Bible does and does not interact with science, and by appreciating the deeper historical and cultural context of the passage, I came to understand Genesis 1 through a figurative lens. I do not think that the Bible teaches that God created the world in six days, 6,000 years ago.

It has been important to me to find an interpretation of the creation account that does not contradict what I hold to be true about the world; a resolution of the tension between Scripture and science protects and enhances my trust in God's Word. More importantly, having a scientifically viable, biblically sound, and theologically vibrant interpretation of Genesis 1 is crucial for the church.

Of course, I'm not saying that all Christians need to adopt a figurative reading of Genesis 1. And clearly, YEC pastors should argue for the merits of their position and preach their consciences. Rather, I'm saying that a responsible figurative interpretation should be acknowledged as the viable alternative that it is.

While we shouldn't compromise our beliefs for the sake of fitting in with unbelievers, neither should we put unnecessary obstacles in their path to God. And the fact is that for many unbelievers, a literal interpretation is just not going to float. Augustine wrote passionately about this issue a long time ago. A well-known quote from him on the matter may sound uncharitable to the modern ear and in any event is very long, so I will merely paraphrase it: An unbeliever has a baseline understanding about the features of the world around him, such as the earth, the sky, and the stars. He feels certain about his elementary knowledge of the world because of his reason and experience. When the unbeliever hears a Christian saying that the Bible teaches things that contradict the unbeliever's reason and experience, he will lose trust in what the Christian says. The unbeliever will then be less likely to believe the Christian on matters such as the resurrection and the kingdom of God.[7] Augustine was concerned that the church would lose credibility in the minds of unbelievers, who would then be less likely to accept Christ. Augustine's concern merits attention today.

We must not create a logical impasse that causes scientifically minded folks to not only reject the teaching of six-day creation, but also the far more central claims of Jesus's divinity, atonement, and resurrection. Young earth creationism advocates teach that the only acceptable way to understand Genesis 1 is as a literal, historical account. Then they assert—correctly, I believe—that the Bible tells a complete, internally consistent story, such that if you take away one piece of it you are removing a foundation for other pieces. The implication is that if Genesis 1 is false, then the foundation for the New Testament is weakened. Sometimes the message is more explicit: If Genesis 1 is not literal history, some argue, then we have no basis to claim that the resurrection literally happened.

Now, if an unbeliever is made to think that Genesis 1 can only be interpreted to mean that the world was created 6,000 years ago in 144 hours, then the unbeliever will conclude that Genesis 1 is a false, untrustworthy account, and perhaps begin to question the validity of the New Testament as well.

To put it a slightly different way: If we tell unbelievers that in order to believe that Genesis 1 is true, they have to believe that God created the world in six days, 6,000 years ago, then many will conclude that Genesis 1 is false. If they believe that Genesis 1 is false, they will have a harder time believing that the rest of the Bible is true. After all, if one part is false, how can they trust the rest?

I respect that YEC advocates are honest and fervent in their defense of the Bible. But in some instances, their efforts can be counterproductive to evangelism. When unbelievers are told that Christianity depends on every verse of Scripture being literally true, their inability to believe in a young earth may lead them to doubt or reject a gospel they'd otherwise embrace! A young woman exploring Christianity may respond to YEC claims by saying to herself, "Well, I don't believe that early Genesis is literal history, so perhaps I shouldn't believe in Jesus either."

I suspect that the scenario I just gave is not uncommon. According to a recent study,[8] "most Americans (59%) say science and religion are often in conflict," including "nearly three-quarters (73%) of those who seldom or never attend worship services." And in a separate study, 70% of young adults ages 18–23 agree that "the teachings of science and religion often ultimately conflict with each other."[9] If unbelievers, including young folks, believe that the Bible teaches things that they feel certain are not true, then they will be less open to submitting to Christ. When it comes to church growth and vitality, the fruit produced through the zeal, passion, and witness of faithful followers of Christ may not fully ripen if the church insists on strict adherence to YEC teaching.

It is vital that we stress to unbelievers that the entire Bible is true, and also that they do not need to believe that a young earth and six-day creation are clear biblical teachings. Fortunately, as I learned and will show in the upcoming chapters, we have a better way to interpret Genesis 1 that does not result in conflicts with science.

This issue affects those in the church as well. In the course of my research for this book, I have come across many testimonials of people who were raised as Christians and had considered themselves to be Christian, but who left the church over conflicts with science. Typically, they had grown up in a YEC home, attended a YEC church, and internalized YEC teaching. Then, when they were inevitably prompted for one reason or another to critically consider their YEC views, they realized that they had to give them up. Since young earth creationism was imbedded so deeply into their Christian worldview, they left the church as well. Some later returned. Some did not.

Even among those who never leave the church, this issue has real import. Christians have legitimate struggles with science and faith issues. Some, perhaps many, Christians live with a level of cognitive dissonance between what they believe to be true about the world and what they think or are told the Bible teaches. For as long as that cognitive dissonance persists—even if it is suppressed or ignored—it may be hindering those believers' spiritual development and interfering with the full enjoyment of their relationship with their Creator.

Finally, when Christians who cannot intellectually accept a young earth are persuaded that Genesis 1 may only be read literally, they may respond by doubting God's Word. They may conclude that the first chapter of the Bible is not truth. This is dangerous and very unfortunate. Once the truth of Genesis 1 is discounted, it is tempting to discount the truth of other difficult parts of the Bible as well. We should be assuring our Christian brethren that they may believe the earth is old without disbelieving the Bible. It will comfort their hearts to know that there is a way to responsibly interpret Genesis 1 that respects the authority of Scripture without leading to a conflict with science.

The journey toward this interpretation begins by examining the conflict between the literal reading of Genesis 1 and modern science. I invite you to walk with me.

Notes

6   Biologos Editorial Team, "A Survey of Clergy and Their Views on Origins," Biologos, accessed September 7, 2019, https://biologos.org/articles/a-survey-of-clergy-and-their-views-on-origins.

7   Augustine, *The Literal Meaning of Genesis,* trans. John Hammond Taylor, S. J. (Mahwah, NJ: Paulist, 1982), 1:42–43.

8   David Masci, "For Darwin Day, 6 facts about the evolution debate," Pew Research Center, accessed September 7, 2019, https://www.pewresearch.org/fact-tank/2019/02/11/darwin-day.

9   Christian Smith, *Souls in Transition* (Oxford: Oxford University Press, 2009), 139.

CHAPTER 4

....

The Basis of YEC Claims

What biblical passages support the YEC claim that the earth is only 6,000 years old? The Genesis 1 creation account provides some context, but the main support comes from the genealogies found throughout the Bible.

Let's take a minute to introduce the biblical genealogies. For example, in the first chapter of his Gospel, Matthew traces the family line of Jesus back to Abraham. Luke 3 gives a genealogy from Jesus back to Adam. Genesis 5 names Adam's descendants to Noah, and Genesis 11 traces Noah's lineage through his son Shem down to Abram. There are other genealogies throughout the Bible as well.

The two Genesis genealogies I mentioned include people's ages. Many of these ages, especially of those who lived before the flood, are extremely old. The oldest person listed is Methuselah, who is said to have lived for 969 years: "When Methuselah had lived 187 years, he fathered Lamech. Methuselah lived after he fathered Lamech 782 years and had other sons and daughters. Thus all the days of Methuselah were 969 years, and he died" (Genesis 5:25–27).

A strict accounting of the genealogies—basically, using the number of people in a genealogy and the given or presumed ages of parenthood, and merely counting back in time to Genesis 1:1—leads to an age of the earth and universe of about 6,000 years. James Ussher

(1581–1656), an Irish archbishop, famously placed the date of creation at October 22, 4004 BC. Others came up with similar dates. Some YEC advocates acknowledge gaps in the genealogies but still hold to a timeline of no more than 10,000 years. I will have more to say about the genealogies later.

The insistence on a creation timeline of six 24-hour days comes from a concrete reading of Genesis 1. In verse 5 we read, "And there was evening and there was morning, the first day." This becomes a pattern, continuing and repeated for six days, concluding in verse 31: "And there was evening and there was morning, the sixth day." This produces a week in which all of creation takes place. I will soon dissect the claim that Genesis 1 portrays a 144-hour workweek.

Other types of supporting evidence include appeals to church history and arguments that some Scripture verses outside of Genesis 1 buttress YEC claims. Personally, church tradition is rarely the paramount consideration for me in Scriptural interpretation, especially when scientific claims are involved. The early church fathers just didn't have the information that we have today. With respect to Scripture passages outside of Genesis 1 that purportedly bear on the age of the earth, I will address that concern at the end of my discussion of creation.

CHAPTER 5

....

The Earth Is Old

It is clear to me that the universe and the earth are not merely 6,000 to 10,000 years old. The current scientific estimates are that the universe is about 13,800,000,000 years old and that the earth is about 4,500,000,000 years old. Evidence that the universe and earth are older than 10,000 years comes from a variety of independent sources.

One piece of information that helps cosmologists place the age of the universe at 13.8 billion years is the speed of light, which is about 182,000 miles per second.[10] Because light takes time to travel, when we see an object, we are actually seeing it as it was in the past. In everyday life, this lag is infinitesimal. But in astronomy, it can be enormous. If we know the distance between us and, say, a distant star, then the speed of light allows us to calculate how far back in history we are observing that star. "When you look out in space, you're looking back into time. The farther across space you look, the further back in time you see."[11] Since we know the distance of very far away objects, we can measure how far back in time we are seeing them.

Another means of dating the universe takes advantage of the fact that it is expanding; celestial objects are getting farther away from us. We can measure how quickly it is expanding, then use math to put that process into reverse and calculate how long it would take for all matter to reach the same point—thus establishing the moment of the Big Bang. As expressed by Hugh Ross, Christian scientist and leader of the organization Reasons to Believe, "The spreading apart of galaxies through time provides direct evidence of the continuous expansion of the universe from an infinitesimal volume."[12] "The maths," as my British friends would say, reveal a universe that is very old indeed.

To see that the earth is older than 10,000 years, we don't need space telescopes or other high-tech methods. James Hutton (1726–1797), known as the Father of Geology, observed that the features of the world around him, be they a coastline or a cliff, were the result of continuous cycles of sedimentation and erosion. Further, these processes took so long that the geology he observed could only be explained in the context of a very old earth.[13] Deserts are a good example of an environment that takes a long time to develop. As Christian geologist Davis Young notes, "It takes time, of course, to erode bedrock to a sandy condition and to blow the material into dunes."[14]

Although we don't strictly need it, there are plenty of data within modern science that establish an old earth. We can obtain an upper boundary on the age of the earth by dating the age of our solar system, which is just a part of the universe. The oldest meteorites found on earth, which presumably formed at the time of the birth of the solar system and arrived on earth afterward, have been dated at 4.53 to 4.58 billion years old.[15, 16] A lower boundary is found by measuring the age of the oldest rocks and crystals found on earth. These are in Western Australia and have an age of 4.3 billion years.[17] It is likely that the earth is older than this. For one thing, it is expected that there were rocks that existed prior to 4.3 billion years ago but were destroyed through tectonic activity or have not been found yet. Also, we have moon rocks, obtained from NASA missions, which have been dated at 4.4 billion to 4.5 billion years of age.[18] We believe that the moon is a little younger than the earth, having been formed by a "titanic collision between the newborn Earth and a Mars-sized object referred to as Theia."[19] The current best estimate for the age of the earth is thus about 4.5 billion years.

At this point a discussion of radiometric dating is warranted, as this technique is responsible for much of the evidence of the age of the earth. Some of the elements that make up rocks and other matter are not stable. These unstable radioactive isotopes decay—losing atoms and thereby some of their weight—and do so at a predictable rate. If you know the starting composition of a sample (when the rock formed) and the ending (present) composition, then you can calculate how much decomposition has taken place. If you then know the speed at which the decomposition happens, you can measure how much time has elapsed since the rock's formation.[20]

As Davis Young notes, it is usually possible to make an estimate of the starting composition of a sample.[21] The details vary by type of dating method. As an example, consider potassium-argon dating. The radioactive potassium isotope produces argon and calcium in a fixed and known proportion when it decays. Argon, as an inert gas, would not have been in the rock when it was formed. Any argon in the rock is a byproduct of decay. So by measuring the amount of potassium present and the amount of argon present you can calculate the amount of potassium originally present. Other dating methods have their own mechanisms for determining the starting composition. And there is also the rubidium-strontium isochron method, where the starting composition does not need to be estimated because it can be calculated directly.[22]

The ending composition can be measured directly. What happens in between the original composition and the ending composition is the decay process. Radioactive parent atoms decay until they become stable daughter atoms. Each unit of decay leads to one less parent atom and one more daughter atom. Christopher Rupe explains the process well using the analogy of an hourglass, with the parent decaying into the daughter steadily over time.[23]

A key to the dating process is knowing how fast the decay progresses—the rate at which the sand in the hourglass moves from the top to the bottom. Fortunately this speed is known. Indeed, "all physical evidence pertaining to decay constants indicates the virtual immutability of those constants."[24] If you divide the amount of decomposition by the rate at which it occurs, you arrive at the time that has elapsed.

There are different types of radiometric dating, as there are many different elements that naturally decay. The most commonly used type is radiocarbon dating. Others include uranium-235, uranium-238, and the aforementioned potassium-argon and rubidium-strontium methods. Radiometric dating is accepted as being very reliable. As Christian geologist Roger Wiens writes:

Radiometric dating—the process of determining the age of rocks from the decay of their radioactive elements—has been in widespread use for over half a century. There are over forty such techniques, each using a different radioactive element or a different way of measuring them. It has become increasingly clear that these radiometric dating techniques agree with each other and as a whole, present a coherent picture in which the Earth was created a very long time ago. Further evidence comes from the complete agreement between radiometric dates and other dating methods such as counting tree rings or glacier ice core layers. Many Christians have been led to distrust radiometric dating and are completely unaware of the great number of laboratory measurements that have shown these methods to be consistent. Many are also unaware that Bible-believing Christians are among those actively involved in radiometric dating.[25]

One particular criticism that I've heard from the YEC community is that radiocarbon dating is not reliable for measuring things that are older than a certain number of years. This is true. Since the half-life of carbon is relatively short, radiocarbon dating loses reliability after 60,000 years or so. However, other isotopes have far longer half-lives. For example, uranium-lead dating can be used to accurately measure samples that are billions of years old.

Returning to the evidence, tree rings also show us that the earth is not young. By counting rings, we can tell how old a tree is. This method has been cross-tested and found to be consistent with the results of carbon dating. Among the oldest trees in the USA are bristlecone pines in Nevada, which go back 4,800 years. When dead trees are preserved via petrification, these older tree rings can be appended to those of the living trees to produce a longer timeline. As Steve Webb writes, "Such age-dating has been done with great confidence and repeatability back to 10,800 years in oak and pine trees in Poland."[26]

Lake varves are similar to tree rings. Each winter and summer season, in lakes that freeze in winter, contrasting layers of sediments form at the bottom of the lake. These can be counted to determine age since, under ideal circumstances, only two layers form per year.[27] One such lake with ideal circumstances is located in Japan, and provides a deposit record of over 50,000 years.[28]

Ice cores also reveal that the earth is old. In parts of Antarctica and Greenland, ice layers form every season or year on top of the previous layer. For relatively young ice cores, layers can be counted, much like tree rings. For older ice cores, radiometric analysis can be used on gases trapped in the ice. This second method was used to show that a recently excavated ice core in Antarctica contains ice that is 2.7 million years old.[29]

Plate tectonics also provides evidence for an old earth. Basically, mountains grow as plates in the earth's crust shift. This growth occurs steadily over a very long period of time. Given Mount Everest's growth rate of half an inch per year, we see that it has been developing for far longer than the 10,000 years allotted by the young-earth model.

Dinosaur bones also point to an old earth. We have found a lot of them, and many are dated to more than 200 million years of age. Furthermore, we have fossil evidence of aquatic unicellular life from billions of years ago.[30] The fossil record in general provides strong evidence of an old earth and also shows that animals and plants existed long before humans.

Coral reefs provide yet another reference point for the age of the earth. Getting an approximate age for a coral reef is simply a matter of dividing its height by its growth per year. Living corals are colonies of animals that inhabit shells made out of calcium carbonate. The growth rate is dependent upon extracting dissolved calcium carbonate from the ocean, and there just isn't a lot of dissolved calcium carbonate (which is quite insoluble) in ocean water. So coral reefs grow just a fraction of an inch per year. A group of coral reefs in the Pacific, called the Eniwetok, appears to be 200,000 to 300,000 years old, and portions of the Grand Bahama Reef appear to be close to 800,000 years old.[31]

Genetic science also points to an old earth. Analysis of the human genome reveals that our species has been around longer than 10,000 years. One dating method uses the "molecular clock." Molecular clock analysis "estimates the timing of humanity's origin and spread around the globe."[32] Geneticists first estimate the rate at which mutations in DNA occur, then the amount of mutations that have accumulated in the human genome over time; with this data, they can estimate how long we have been in existence as a species.

The above is an incomplete list of the available evidence for an old earth, but I trust it is enough to make my point. It is certainly no exaggeration to say, as Ken Miller does, that "young-earth creationism requires a full frontal assault on virtually every field of modern science."[33]

Young earth creationists respond with various objections, of which I'll mention but a couple. One is the "apparent age" theory that God created the world with an appearance of age by giving light from distant stars a head start toward earth and by creating apparently old geological formations. I simply don't find that argument to be credible. It would imply, for instance, that God placed in the ground bones of dinosaurs that never actually lived. Another YEC assertion is that the laws of physics—or at least the values of important parameters— changed after the flood. Yet as David Snoke points out, "One cannot change the values of any of the constants of nature by more than a fraction of a percent without making life as we know it impossible. For example, the energy emitted by the sun depends sensitively on the speed of light; if the speed were a little faster, the sun would burn out rapidly."[34] Likewise, I dismiss conspiracy theories out of hand. As Justin Barrett relates,

Conspiracy theories about scientists piecing together ordinary bits of bone to make dinosaurs or relying on faulty radiocarbon dating techniques to argue that the earth was hundreds of millions of years old became increasingly absurd once I got to know science and scientists firsthand. The degree to which they are willing to publicly fight each other over seemingly trivial matters, the way jealousy and competitiveness leads to savage personal integrity attacks and the fierce independence of many scientists all make widespread conspiracies very unlikely indeed.[35]

It seems to me that God's book of nature tells us that the heavens and the earth were created much more than 10,000 years ago. The age of the earth is one area where we should let our scientific knowledge assist us in our biblical interpretation.

Notes

10   Carolyn Collins Petersen, *Astronomy 101* (Avon, MA: Adams Media, 2017), 14.

11   Petersen, 14.

12   Hugh Ross, *More Than a Theory* (Grand Rapids, MI: Baker Books, 2009), 56.

13   James Hutton, *Theory of the Earth* (New York: Classic Books International, 2010), 83–90.

14   Davis A. Young, *Christianity and the Age of the Earth* (Muskogee, OK: Artisan, 2014), 91.

15   "Age of the Earth," US Geological Survey (USGS), accessed September 24, 2019, http://pubs.usgs.gov/gip/geotime/age.html.

16   Note, as an aside, that the sun is considered to have been formed at the beginning of the solar system and is thus also estimated to have been created billions of years ago.

17   "Age of the Earth," US Geological Survey (USGS).

18   Susan Benecchi, Paula Gossard, and Gladys Kober, *The Crossroads of Science and Faith: Astronomy Through a Christian Worldview* (n.p.: Glimpse of His Splendor, 2015), 243.

19   Petersen, *Astronomy 101*, 50.

20   Frank Steiger, "Radioactive Dating," Tufts University, accessed March 26, 2020, http://chem.tufts.edu/science/FrankSteiger/radioact.htm.

21   Davis A. Young, *Christianity and the Age of the Earth*, 98.

22   Davis A. Young, *Creation and the Flood* (Grand Rapids, MI: Baker Books, 1977), 185–90.

23   Christopher Rupe and John Sanford, *Contested Bones* (n.p.: FMS, 2019), 271.

24   Davis A. Young and Ralph F. Stearley, *The Bible, Rocks, and Time* (Downers Grove, IL: IVP Academic, 2008), 473.

25   Roger C. Wiens, "Radiometric Dating: A Christian Perspective," The American Scientific Affiliation, last modified 2002, https://www.asa3.org/ASA/resources/Wiens.html.

26   Steve Webb, "The Age of the Earth Part 4: Glacial Varves and Tree Rings," Blogos, accessed September 7, 2019, http://www.blogos.org/scienceandtechnology/age-earth-tree-rings.php.

27   Bernd Zolitschka et al., "Varves in lake sediments—a review," *Quaternary Science Reviews*, 117 (2015): 1–41.

28   R. Joel Duff, "Lake Suigetsu and the 60,000 Year Varve Chronology," *Naturalis Historia*, November 12, 2012, https://thenaturalhistorian.com/2012/11/12/varves-chronologysuigetsu-c14-radiocarbon-callibration-creationism.

29   Paul Voosen, "Record-shattering 2.7-million-year-old ice core reveals start of the ice ages," last modified August 15, 2017, *Science*, https://www.sciencemag.org/news/2017/08/record-shattering-27-million-year-old-ice-core-reveals-start-ice-ages.

30   Michael J. Benton and David A. T. Harper, *Introduction to Paleobiology and the Fossil Record* (Oxford: Wiley Blackwell, 2009), 191.

31   Perry G. Phillips, "Coral Reefs: Indicators of an Old Earth," The American Scientific Affiliation, accessed September 7, 2019, https://www.asa3.org/ASA/education/origins/coralreefs.htm.

32   Fazale Rana, *Who Was Adam?* (Colorado Springs: NavPress, 2005), 59.

33   Kenneth R. Miller, *Finding Darwin's God* (New York: Harper Perennial, 2007), 81.

34   David Snoke, *A Biblical Case for an Old Earth* (Grand Rapids, MI: Baker Books, 2006), 28.

35   Justin L. Barrett in *How I Changed My Mind About Evolution*, eds. Kathryn Applegate and J.B. Stump (Downers Grove, IL: InterVarsity, 2016), 140.

CHAPTER 6

....

Opening the Bible

What then? Is there a contradiction between the book of Scripture and the book of nature? Well, when the Bible and science appear to be in conflict, then the interpretation of one or both is in error. We've seen that it is very unlikely that so much independently generated science is dead wrong. So if the science is likely not as wrong as it would have to be to accommodate the YEC view, then it is likely that the YEC interpretation of Scripture is in error. How then should we interpret Genesis 1? Let's investigate. We'll start with the text, apply a literal interpretation to see if that fits, and if not, then try figurative meanings. As a quick note, the relevant passage actually extends into chapter 2 (Genesis 1:1–2:3), but for simplicity we'll continue to refer to it as Genesis 1.

1:1In the beginning, God created the heavens and the earth. 2The earth was without form and void, and darkness was over the face of the deep. And the Spirit of God was hovering over the face of the waters.

3And God said, "Let there be light," and there was light. 4And God saw that the light was good. And God separated the light from the darkness. 5God called the light Day, and the darkness he called Night. And there was evening and there was morning, the first day.

⁶And God said, "Let there be an expanse in the midst of the waters, and let it separate the waters from the waters." ⁷And God made the expanse and separated the waters that were under the expanse from the waters that were above the expanse. And it was so. ⁸And God called the expanse Heaven. And there was evening and there was morning, the second day.

⁹And God said, "Let the waters under the heavens be gathered together into one place, and let the dry land appear." And it was so. ¹⁰God called the dry land Earth, and the waters that were gathered together he called Seas. And God saw that it was good.

¹¹And God said, "Let the earth sprout vegetation, plants yielding seed, and fruit trees bearing fruit in which is their seed, each according to its kind, on the earth." And it was so. ¹²The earth brought forth vegetation, plants yielding seed according to their own kinds, and trees bearing fruit in which is their seed, each according to its kind. And God saw that it was good. ¹³And there was evening and there was morning, the third day.

¹⁴And God said, "Let there be lights in the expanse of the heavens to separate the day from the night. And let them be for signs and for seasons, and for days and years, ¹⁵and let them be lights in the expanse of the heavens to give light upon the earth." And it was so. ¹⁶And God made the two great lights—the greater light to rule the day and the lesser light to rule the night—and the stars. ¹⁷And God set them in the expanse of the heavens to give light on the earth, ¹⁸to rule over the day and over the night, and to separate the light from the darkness. And God saw that it was good. ¹⁹And there was evening and there was morning, the fourth day.

²⁰And God said, "Let the waters swarm with swarms of living creatures, and let birds fly above the earth across the expanse of the heavens." ²¹So God created the great sea creatures and every living creature that moves, with which the waters swarm, according to their kinds, and every winged bird according to its kind. And God saw that it was good. ²²And God blessed them, saying, "Be fruitful and multiply and fill the waters in the seas, and let birds multiply on the earth." ²³And there was evening and there was morning, the fifth day.

²⁴And God said, "Let the earth bring forth living creatures according to their kinds—livestock and creeping things and beasts of the earth according to their kinds." And it was so. ²⁵And God made the beasts of the earth according to their kinds and the livestock according to their kinds, and everything that creeps on the ground according to its kind. And God saw that it was good.

²⁶Then God said, "Let us make man in our image, after our likeness. And let them have dominion over the fish of the sea and over the birds of the heavens and over the livestock and over all the earth and over every creeping thing that creeps on the earth." ²⁷So God created man in his own image, in the image of God he created him; male and female he created them.

²⁸And God blessed them. And God said to them, "Be fruitful and multiply and fill the earth and subdue it, and have dominion over the fish of the sea and over the birds of the heavens and over every living thing that moves on the earth." ²⁹And God said, "Behold, I have given you every plant yielding seed that is on the face of all the earth, and every tree with seed in its fruit. You shall have them for food. ³⁰And to every beast of the earth and to every bird of the heavens and to everything that creeps on the

earth, everything that has the breath of life, I have given every green plant for food." And it was so. [31]*And God saw everything that he had made, and behold, it was very good. And there was evening and there was morning, the sixth day.*

[2:1]*Thus the heavens and the earth were finished, and all the host of them.* [2]*And on the seventh day God finished his work that he had done, and he rested on the seventh day from all his work that he had done.* [3]*So God blessed the seventh day and made it holy, because on it God rested from all his work that he had done in creation.*

The first thing to recognize is that the language is anything but plain. This text is hard to decipher. Even just the first verse is problematic. Is it a summary, an introduction of the passage that follows, or does the verse describe an act of creation that predates the rest of the passage? The second verse is even more difficult. What does it mean that the earth was without form and void? What is the deep? Going a little further, what is the "expanse in the midst of the waters"? And as for the days, I concur with Augustine, who wrote, "What kind of days these were it is extremely difficult, or perhaps impossible for us to conceive, and how much more to say!"[36] For example, it seems that the sun was created in day four, but how then was there light in day one? How did plant life sprout up in day three without a sun!? I am not alone in being perplexed by a literal interpretation of this passage. Genesis 1 has been flummoxing readers for millennia.

No, the text is anything but plain. Indeed, throughout church history, Christianity's brightest minds have struggled with this passage. Even in pre-modern times, there was much disagreement on whether creation took place in six 24-hour days. Robert Letham rightly asks, "If the text of Genesis is so clear-cut why did the church down the centuries not see it that way? Does that not say something not only about the interpreters but also the text?"[37]

The majority view seems to have been that of a literal account, akin to current YEC beliefs. For example, "Luther and Calvin give preference to a literal reading of the days."[38] Many theologians, however, had other views. As John Lennox discusses,[39] Philo and Augustine thought creation was the act of a moment, which occurred in Genesis 1:1. For Philo, the Genesis record had more to do with principles of order and arrangement. Justin Martyr suggested that days may have been long epochs. Clement of Alexandria argued that creation could not take place in time at all, because time as we understand it did not exist before the world was created. And Origen wrote in a seemingly snarky tone, "Now what man of intelligence will believe that the first and the second and third day, and the evening and the morning existed without the sun and moon and stars? And that the first day, if we may so call it, was even without a heaven?"[40] I think Peter Enns sums it up well when he remarks, "Genesis is not now and never has been an easy book to understand. It raises its own questions and requires skill and learning to handle well; thoughtful people have been doing that since long before the modern era."[41] Yes indeed, and we need to be thoughtful—and cautious—as we tackle the text.

Notes

36 Augustine, *The City of God* (New York: Random House, 1993), 350.

37 Robert Letham, "'In the Space of Six Days': The Days of Creation from Origen to the Westminster Assembly," *Westminster Theological Journal* 61 (1999): 149–74.

38 Jennifer Powell McNutt in *Since the Beginning*, ed. Kyle R. Greenwood (Grand Rapids, MI: Baker, 2018), 194.

39 John C. Lennox, *Seven Days that Divide the World* (Grand Rapids, MI: Zondervan, 2011), 41.

40 Quoted from *De principiis IV.iii.1* by Keith D. Stanglin in "Reading Genesis with the Church," April 12, 2017, https://henrycenter.tiu.edu/2017/04/reading-genesis-with-thechurch.

41 Peter Enns, *The Evolution of Adam* (Grand Rapids, MI: Brazos, 2012), 12.

CHAPTER 7

....

A Literal Approach

In my hope to reconcile science with Scripture, the first approach I took was to read Genesis concretely to see if perhaps a close examination would yield an interpretation that allowed for an old earth. What follows is generally called the day-age theory, championed by old earth creationism (OEC) advocates. OEC advocates believe that a literal reading of Genesis 1 is warranted and reveals accurate scientific information about how God created the universe and the earth and everything in it over the course of billions of years. A handy place to go to summarize this theory is Rich Deem's website godandscience.org.[42] I found, to my surprise, that there is a reasonable case to be made that a concrete reading teaches an old earth. At first, I was excited and cautiously optimistic about the OEC interpretation. However, as I delved deeper into it, I bumped into several apparent difficulties and contradictions. Many reasonable thinkers may agree with the OEC interpretation, but in the end, several aspects were just not fully convincing to me.

One helpful thing that I learned from my OEC research is that the genealogies may contain gaps and therefore can cover a longer period of time than a surface reading would suggest. The reason for this is that when the Bible says "A begat B," B is not necessarily the son of A. B could be, for example, a great, great grandson. It is widely accepted that some gaps are present. In fact, this becomes self-apparent when we begin comparing the genealogies side by side: we see that one has intermediate members. As such, we cannot use the genealogies to determine the age of the earth. An example or two will help. In Matthew 1:8 we read that Joram was the father of Uzziah. Yet in 1 Chronicles 3:11–12 we see that Joram was the father of Ahaziah, who was the father of Joash, who was the father of *Amaziah*. Now Amaziah was also known as Uzziah, as we can see by comparing 2 Kings 14:21–22 with 2 Chronicles 26:1–2. So Matthew skipped a couple of generations. Another example is given by comparing Matthew 1:11, which states that Josiah was the father of Jechoniah, with 1 Chronicles 3:15–16, which describes Josiah as the grandfather of Jeconiah (slight difference in spelling but the same person).

Many YEC advocates accept the existence of gaps yet argue that it is unrealistic to use them to stretch the timeline past 10,000 years. The question really becomes how many gaps, and of what length, we can expect to have in the timeline. I don't see any reason why, in theory, the gaps could not be very large. Think about it this way: If the complete actual genealogy indeed stretched out over an extremely long period of time, and if the genealogies were passed down by oral tradition prior to being written, wouldn't it make sense that the written record should contain only a small sample of the most prominent and significant members of the line, rather than the full accounting? Still, though, "stretching" the genealogies all the way back to the appearance of humanity means going back tens, even hundreds, of millennia; that seems like a tall order. I'll have more to say on the genealogies later on.

A second thing I discovered is that the exact meaning of the word "day" in the text is actually not so clear. Ancient Hebrew had a very small vocabulary, perhaps as small as 3,000 words.[43] As a result, many words have multiple meanings. In Genesis 1, the word from which we get "day" is *yom*. Throughout the Bible, yom often means a strict 24-hour day but has other meanings as well. Importantly, a long, indeterminate period of time is one of those other meanings.

There are many instances in the Old Testament where yom refers to an indefinite period of time, although "the examples generally used of yom referring to an extended period of time are examples in which the word is being used idiomatically: 'in that day.'"[44] So, the "days" of Genesis 1 could refer to very long periods of time. And it is worth noting that there is no evening and morning mentioned on day seven, so day seven especially could have been a very long time.

Ah, but there we have that phrase "and there was evening and there was morning" for the six creation days. Could this be consistent with an old earth? Well, it could serve as a bracket to each day, signifying that each day, although extremely long, had a beginning and an end. But if this were the case, we would expect the beginning, morning, to come before the end, evening. Instead, we have "and there was evening (end) and there was morning (beginning)." Alternatively, the whole phrase "and there was evening and there was morning" could refer to the nighttime, the end of the day. The phrase could signify that each day had an end—in other words, that there were separate days, each of indeterminate length. So if we work a bit we can view the phrase in a manner that fits the OEC view by construing a day to be an extremely long period of time. The natural reading of the text, though, does seem to imply regular 24-hour days.

OEC advocates argue that the order of creation in Genesis 1 matches quite well with what we know from modern science. There are some intriguing similarities, but in the end I was unconvinced and became dissatisfied with the concrete interpretation of Genesis 1. Let's go through Genesis 1, piece by piece, and analyze the OEC perspective.

Genesis 1:1 states, "In the beginning, God created the heavens and the earth." Plausibly, this corresponds well with the period of time starting with the instantaneous initial creation of the universe and continuing through the formation of the earth. David Snoke sets "the Big Bang at the very first line of Genesis."[45] John Lennox sees things similarly, commenting that "the Standard (Big Bang) Model developed by physicists and cosmologists can be seen as a scientific unpacking of the implications of the statement, 'In the beginning God created the heavens and the earth.'"[46] Note also that the heavens are mentioned first, which fits the scientific timeline. In this rendering, the initial creation of the universe and the earth occurred prior to, or at the beginning of, day one. A good case is made by Rich Deem:

When we look at Genesis 1:2, we see that it begins with the conjunction "and." This fact immediately tells us that Genesis 1:1 and 1:2 are part of one continuous thought. Remove the period at the end of Genesis 1:1 and read it as originally intended: In the beginning, God created the heavens and the earth and the earth was formless and void. ... The conjunction at the beginning of Genesis 1:2 tells us that Genesis 1:1 is not a summary of the creation account! This verse is a factual statement of what God did at the beginning of the first day.[47]

A majority of scholars do, however, view Genesis 1:1 as being an introduction to the rest of the chapter rather than a first act of creation. To my mind, the natural reading of Genesis 1:1 seems to make it an introduction, and a closer inspection of the text adds weight to this view. I'll have more to say on this later, but for now I'll just point out the symmetry between the beginning of the creation account (Genesis 1:1) and its end (Genesis 2:1–3). In Genesis 1:1, the order is *God, created,* and then *heavens and earth.* In Genesis 2:1–3, the order is reversed. *Heavens and earth* is mentioned first, then *finished,* and then *God.* This suggests that Genesis 1:1 and 2:1–3 are bookends of the creation account, with Genesis 1:1 being the introduction. And actually, Genesis is full of introductions. There are 11 *toledots,* or "accounts," that begin with an introduction, such as Genesis 5:1 ("This is the book of the generations of Adam").[48] Generally, there follows a genealogy, then a story or stories about one or more of the people in the genealogy. The book of Genesis is structured around these toledots.

Genesis 1:2 reads, "The earth was without form and void, and darkness was over the face of the deep. And the Spirit of God was hovering over the face of the waters." This could correspond with the state of the earth relatively early in its existence. Long ago, the atmosphere was very dense, such that it may have been quite dark; the globe was completely covered by water as plate tectonics and volcanic activity had not yet pushed the continents up above sea level; and the first life forms (unicellular marine organisms) had yet to appear. As Hugh Ross comments, "Observational data, including the study of the Earth's oldest rocks, and theoretical modeling of planetary formation together verify the historical accuracy of early Earth's conditions described in Genesis 1:2. Water did, indeed, initially cover all of the Earth's crust."[49] This interpretation seems plausible to me but leaves unanswered questions. For example, if the atmosphere had been thinner, would there have been light? In other words, was the sun created in Genesis 1:1?

"Let there be light" in Genesis 1:3 could refer to the point where the atmosphere thinned out enough such that the sun's light penetrated down to the surface of the earth. This would have produced, from the perspective of an observer on the surface of the earth, a day/night light cycle, such that the light and darkness were separated. Again, this is a plausible interpretation, but I don't think it really fits the text. The text is quite dramatic and seems to imply an instantaneous event rather than a gradual process. In the OEC telling, however, it would have been such a gradual process that the first light would have been barely perceptible, like the first faintest hints of dawn before the sun peeks up above the horizon. And where is the light coming from? Perhaps a temporary light source, but the text is silent on this. Or the sun could have been created as part of the heavens in Genesis 1:1, but the text does not give supporting evidence of this, and as I've mentioned, I think that Genesis 1:1 is an introductory overview. So again, the OEC interpretation seems like a stretch to me.

The separation of the waters on day two could be the creation of a water cycle, with clouds dropping rain which then evaporates and returns to the clouds. However, the Hebrew word translated "expanse" in the ESV is *raqiya*. Many translations render the word as something firm and solid. The NIV renders it "vault," the NKJV has "firmament," and the NRSV has "dome." The ESV mentions (in the margin) "vault" as an alternative translation. Scholars are divided. While I've come across multiple scholars who think it should be translated "sky" or something similar,[50] the majority of researchers seem to hold that raqiya refers to something like a "dome," a solid barrier that holds up water above it. For example Denis Lamoureux writes that "Scripture states that God created the firmament to separate the heavenly sea from the earthly sea (day two), and then He placed the sun, moon, and stars in the firmament (day four)."[51] Also Conrad Hyers explains that "*firmament* referred literally to a solid, metallic band believed to stretch across the sky like a cosmic version of a domed stadium."[52] This of course does not comport with modern science, but it does comport with the scientific understanding of the day when Genesis was written. As we'll see later, people at that time believed that there were vast reservoirs of water below the earth based on their observation of springs and rivers. Likewise, they believed there were waters, literally a sea of water, above the earth. It makes sense, given those assumptions, that there would have to be something firm holding up the waters above. So here again, the OEC interpretation seems tenuous.

Moving on with our investigation of the OEC interpretation of Genesis 1, the formation of land on day three corresponds well with the geological history of the earth, where plate tectonics and volcanic activity eventually led to the formation of continents.[53] No problem there. Day three also features the creation of plant life. Here, there are clear problems with the OEC interpretation, namely the timing of the creation of fruit trees, and plants more generally. From the fossil record, we know that fruit trees appear quite recently, well after the appearance of land animals, which are not created until day six.

Even non-fruit bearing trees did not appear in the fossil record until after insects, which are not created until day six, and after fish, which are created in day five. Some OEC advocates argue that the days in Genesis 1 are overlapping, but that obliterates the meaning of the days. Another problem is the existence of plant life in the absence of a sun, which is not created until day four. We've discussed this already, and will turn to the issue again presently in our discussion of day four.

Day four features the sun and the moon and the stars. Genesis 1:16 states that God made (*asah*) the two great lights, and the stars also. This day is quite problematic for the OEC interpretation; it is hard to figure a way in which the plants of day three can exist without the sun, or even how there were days one, two, or three at all without the sun or the moon. OEC advocates claim that the sun, moon, and stars were created in Genesis 1:1 as part of the heavens. This is a plausible interpretation, although as I've explained, I don't buy it. I think, rather, that Genesis 1:1 is an introduction to the chapter. But even if we read Genesis 1:1 as a pre-day-one creation of the heavens and earth, including the sun, moon, and stars, there would seem to be a contradiction. Genesis 1:16 says that the sun, moon, and stars were made on day four. Surely they were not made twice! The OEC advocates have two replies. First, they read "asah" in Genesis 1:16 as referring to past action, based upon the form of the word.[54] Second, they note that asah is used instead of *bara*, and that while bara is mainly used to convey an ex-nihilo creation by God, asah can alternatively mean to fashion or prepare. Thus day four is about God placing the already created objects in the heavens to serve their purposes. This leaves me with a question: If the sun, moon, and stars were created in Genesis 1:1 and merely set in the heavens on day four, then where were they in between, during days one, two, and three? OEC advocates would claim that they were in the heavens but not yet appointed for their purposes. Again, I view this as plausible, yet I am not quite satisfied. It seems to me that the OEC position has to twist and contort to achieve concordance with the text.

Sea and air creatures are the focus of day five. This is the first time that animal life is discussed in the Bible. Strictly speaking, the scientific record reveals that marine life, albeit single-celled life, began earlier than day five. The author could have, quite reasonably, overlooked things such as unicellular life, about which the Israelites would have been unaware. Rich Deem writes,

I would first like to point out that God has not revealed the entire creation process in the Genesis creation account, but only that which is particularly relevant to mankind. Many events in the creation account of the Bible have been intentionally left out (unicellular life forms, dinosaurs, etc.), I believe, because they would have been difficult to express in the Hebrew language, and would have led to confusion, since they would not have been understood through the vast majority of mankind's existence (i.e., only understandable in the last two centuries).[55]

Single-celled organisms and dinosaurs, however, are not the only difficulties with the OEC interpretation of day five. Birds appear in the scientific record after land animals, not before. Likewise, in the fossil record birds appear after insects and worms (day six), a food source for many (but by no means all) birds. The OEC account just doesn't seem to fit together to me, and I feel like I have to squeeze and contort the text and use a bit of mental gymnastics in order to get it to match the science. It seems like OEC advocates are using a pretty big shoehorn to fit science into the Bible.

Animals and humans dominate day six. Most of what I could say about day six—how the order of creation it describes is contradictory to the fossil record—I've already discussed. In the fossil record, land animals and insects appear well before the organisms belonging to earlier days of creation.

In the final analysis, I simply determined that there was too much out of place with the OEC interpretation of Genesis 1. Too many loose ends. Too many questionable interpretive choices. Too many interpretive dilemmas. It seemed like I needed to contort the text and use creative interpretation to get it to match with science. In addition, as I'll discuss soon, I was coming to a strong conviction that the author of Genesis 1 did not intend to convey scientific knowledge.

Notes

42   In particular, Rich Deem, "Does Genesis One Conflict with Science? Day-Age Interpretation," at http://godandscience.org/apologetics/day-age.html.

43   Adam Graham, "Why I Believe In An Old Earth (Part 1): The Text Itself," *No King But Christ* (blog), August 22, 2019, https://www.nokingbutchrist.org/why-i-believe-in-an-old-earth-part-1-the-text-itself.

44   John H. Walton, *The Lost World of Genesis One* (Downers Grove, IL: IVP Academic, 2009), 90.

45   David Snoke, *A Biblical Case for an Old Earth* (Grand Rapids, MI: Baker Books, 2006), 127.

46   John C. Lennox, *Seven Days that Divide the World* (Grand Rapids, MI: Zondervan, 2011), 154.

47   Rich Deem, "The Literal Interpretation of the Genesis One Creation Account," accessed March 24, 2020, http://www.godandscience.org/youngearth/genesis1.html.

48   This takes 36:9 as a separate toledot rather than merely a repetition of 36:1. Many commentators hold that there are ten toledots in Genesis.

49   Hugh Ross, *Navigating Genesis* (Covina, CA: RTB, 2014), 36.

50   For example, William Barrick in *Four Views on the Historical Adam*, eds. Matthew Barrett and Ardel B. Caneday (Grand Rapids, MI: Zondervan, 2013), 81–82. He writes that expanse "offers a superior rendering" and that a solid firmament relies on a "lexicographical fallacy."

51   Denis O. Lamoureux in *Four Views on the Historical Adam*, eds. Matthew Barrett and Ardel B. Caneday (Grand Rapids, MI: Zondervan, 2013), 230.

52   Conrad Hyers, *The Meaning of Creation* (Atlanta: John Knox, 1984), 39.

53   Ross, *Navigating Genesis*, 47.

54   Ross, 54.

55   Rich Deem, "Does Genesis One Conflict with Science? Day-Age Interpretation."

CHAPTER 8

....

Pivoting to a Figurative
Perspective

So where did that leave me? I had rejected the YEC interpretation, and while I had genuine respect for the OEC interpretation, in the end I was not comfortable with it. So that ruled out a concrete, literal interpretation of Genesis 1. As discussed in chapter 2, when literal interpretations do not fit, a good next step is to try a figurative interpretation. And since the Bible is truth, then to the extent that it does not have a literal meaning, the passage must have a nonliteral meaning. At this point, as I was learning more about the Bible, it was beginning to make intuitive sense to me that Genesis 1 would employ figurative devices. I became open-minded on that score and even came to expect the use of metaphor. There were three main reasons for this.

Genre

First, I learned that the genre of Genesis 1 suggests a figurative reading. At about this stage of my investigation, I was learning to appreciate the richness of the literature of the Bible. It really is a library of books with many different genres, from narrative to poetry and just about everything in between. And each biblical genre, I was beginning to understand, gives a specific lens through which we should read the text. For instance poetry, which is often meant to convey an idea or a feeling, should not be interpreted the same way as is narrative, which is often meant to convey information. Ascertaining genre can be difficult, however. For example, some parables read like historical narrative. We don't know whether the parable of the good Samaritan was a literal description of a past event or a stylized story. Perhaps nowhere in the Bible is genre more difficult to discern than it is in Genesis 1–11. And whereas it does not matter whether the parable of the good Samaritan is historical narrative or stylized prose—the message is the same either way—the genre of early Genesis may have some bearing on its message. This is a difficult nut to crack, and it is important not to get it wrong.

Understandably, there is much debate in scholarly circles about the genre of Genesis 1. Many, of course, consider it straightforward history. Many others, however, have a different viewpoint and recognize the challenges of categorizing early Genesis. As Kenneth Mathews notes, "Genesis 1:1–2:3, in fact, does not clearly fit a traditional literary category."[56] Gordon Wenham calls early Genesis "protohistory," which is not ordinary history yet not fiction either.[57] Kenton Sparks characterizes Genesis 1–11 as "ancient historiography," where the intent "was not to precisely relay events that occurred in space and time."[58] John Walton and Tremper Longman III opine that "the genre of Genesis is theological history,"[59] which speaks of events that actually happened, while selecting and interpreting those events according to the purpose of the author. Denis Lamoureux, in a quote he attributes to J.I. Packer, describes Genesis as "written in 'picture language.'"[60] Claus Westermann notes that "(Genesis) 1 contains a fusion of poetry and prose that is unique in the Old Testament."[61] Bruce Waltke opines that "Genesis is literature because it communicates doctrine in an artful way; it is ideological art. The narrator uses words not as a stick but as a web. He teaches by telling stories." Waltke notes that the story of creation in particular is highly patterned and does not read like scientific reporting. "The [daily] process of creation typically follows a pattern of announcement, commandment, separation, report, naming, evaluation, and chronological framework."[62]

From my own standpoint, Genesis 1 is not quite poetry, but not quite narrative prose either. It has a lyrical aspect to it and is deeply concerned with theological questions. The author does not show concern with imparting precise scientific knowledge and has not offered a detailed and scientifically precise account of creation. The account here is similar to narrative, but the language and structure are artful, and the content is highly symbolic. Perhaps it is best described as *sui generis*—its own unique class or type. Whatever the best generic descriptor is, I am confident in naming one thing that it is not: modern journalism. Once I made that determination, I allowed myself to consider figurative interpretations.

Expecting Metaphors

I became further drawn to a figurative interpretation when I considered the value of metaphor. Conceptual metaphors are useful for explaining things that are at the edge of or beyond the limits of the reader's immediate senses, allowing the reader to grasp key concepts.[63] This is a key reason for the use of metaphor in the Bible. Well, the events and subjects of Genesis 1 definitely qualify as "beyond the limits of the immediate senses" of the ancient Near Eastern reader: Creation of the universe? Check. Creation of plant and animal life? Check. The nature of God? Check. God's relationship to the world and to us? Again, check.

I'll also here note a related issue, which is that neither the author nor anyone else was present for the creation, at least until day six. One of the implications of this is that there was neither a written account nor oral tradition of the events. We are talking about primeval history here. This does not deny the possibility that Genesis 1 is a blow-by-blow account—divine revelation could have provided all the details to the author—yet it suggests that we should be on the lookout for metaphorical meaning.

The Bible Is Not a Science Textbook

The third reason why I began to look for a figurative meaning to Genesis 1 was my growing belief that the Holy Spirit did not intend to impart scientific knowledge in the pages of the Bible. He did not teach modern science, and He did not teach ancient science. Thus, He did not teach science at all. We'll explore this in the next chapter.

Notes

56   Kenneth A. Mathews, *Genesis 1–11:26*, The New American Commentary (Nashville: B&H, 1996), 109.

57   Gordon J. Wenham in *Genesis: History, Fiction, or Neither*, ed. Charles Halton (Grand Rapids, MI: Zondervan, 2015), 87.

58   See Charles Halton in *Genesis: History, Fiction, or Neither*, ed. Charles Halton (Grand Rapids, MI: Zondervan, 2015), 156.

59   Tremper Longman III and John H. Walton, *The Lost World of the Flood* (Downers Grove, IL: IVP Academic, 2018), 91.

60   Denis O. Lamoureux in *How I Changed my Mind about Evolution*, eds. Kathryn Applegate and J. B. Stump (Downers Grove, IL: InterVarsity, 2016), 145.

61   Claus Westermann, *Genesis 1–11* (Minneapolis: Fortress, 1994), 90.

62   Bruce K. Waltke, *Genesis* (Grand Rapids, MI: Zondervan Academic, 2001), 31, 56.

63   Christy Hemphill, "All in a Week's Work: Using Conceptual Metaphor Theory to Explain Figurative Meaning in Genesis 1," *Journal of the American Scientific Affiliation* 71, no. 4 (2019): 233–254.

CHAPTER 9

....

The Bible Is Not a
Science Textbook

No Modern Science in the Bible, Part 1

There are several reasons why I believe that the Holy Spirit did not intend to teach modern science. First, leaving aside the controversy over Genesis 1, I know of no place in the Old Testament (or the New Testament, for that matter) where an author introduces a scientific fact that was unknown to his contemporaries. Similarly, John Walton notes,

> *In the pages of Scripture I cannot find one example of God giving revelations about the mechanisms and processes of the ancient world that everyone in the ancient world did not believe. God appears to be content to communicate in terms of what the Israelites believed about the material cosmos. We dare not read our science between the lines lest we intrude on the authority granted to the communicators in the Israelite context.*[64]

In short, if the Holy Spirit intended the Bible to teach modern science, one would expect to see modern science in the Bible. But the best we can find is imagery that happens to invoke modern scientific concepts. One example may be Isaiah 40:22, which speaks of God as one "who stretches out the heavens like a curtain, and spreads them like a tent to dwell in." Some OEC advocates contend that this verse and others like it (e.g. Job 9:8, "who alone stretched out the heavens") speak to the expansion of the universe.[65] I see it as a poetic way of describing the majesty of the sky, which stretches as far as the eye can see, which exhibits the power and glory of God, and which God lovingly created to house His creatures. Furthermore, as discussed earlier, the original readers of the Bible thought that the sky was solid, and while solid metal can be flattened and stretched—for example in turning an ingot into a plate by use of a hammer and anvil (and heat)—it is a stretch, pun intended, to portray metal as expanding infinitely. To me, passages such as this were clearly not written to provide modern readers with a hidden code, nor to teach us what we can easily learn in a textbook.

No Modern Science in the Bible, Part 2

Second, and related to the point above, we can deduce that the Holy Spirit did not intend to teach modern science because when the Bible speaks of science, the authors use the science of the time. As we discussed above, in the ancient Near East culture, the sky was thought to be a solid dome with a sea above the dome. In addition, there were believed to be waters below the earth, along with an underworld where the dead lived. The ancients believed in a three-tiered universe. As Dennis Linscomb summarizes:

Everyone in the ANE (Egyptians, Mesopotamians, Canaanites, Hittites, and Israelites) believed that the universe was in three

*tiers: heavens above, earth in the middle, and the underworld
below the earth. They believed the earth was a single
disk-shaped continent. At the edge of this continent were high
mountains that held up the sky with roots in the underworld.
Cosmic waters flowed all around the cosmos and were held back
by the sky. The earth floated on water, though they believed it
was also supported on pillars. They viewed the sky as a solid
dome. ... The main function of this sky dome was to hold back
the waters above. The stars were engraved on this dome and
moved in tracks.*[66]

Some claim that this depiction of a three-tiered universe was
merely employed in a figurative sense and that there was no literal
belief in, for example, a cosmic sea. Against this, Kyle Greenwood
argues the following:

*There are several reasons we must reject this notion [of a
figurative use]. First, wherever we find physical descriptions of
the cosmos, it is described as three-tiered. Second, wherever we
find iconographic images or drawings of the cosmos, they are
three-tiered. Third, nowhere in the ancient world do we find the
authors explaining their cosmology in any other terms besides
the three-tiered system. Finally, we know that ancients thought
of the cosmos in terms of the heavens, earth, and seas because
eventually these ideas were challenged by Aristotle and Ptolemy,
whose ideas were later challenged by Copernicus, Galileo and
Kepler.*[67]

These ancient conceptions about the earth and the universe
are reflected in the Bible. The Holy Spirit did not correct the faulty
scientific views of the original audience. Instead, He accommodated
to the original audience, assuming the science of the day to more
effectively communicate theological truths. As Arie Leegwater

states, "The Bible speaks in prescientific language and pictures. It employs the language of the day, reflecting the world-picture of the original audience. The language of the Bible is accommodated to the cosmological and historical awareness of the day."[68]

With respect to the solid dome, we already looked at Genesis 1:6, which arguably speaks of this and which also speaks of waters below the firmament and waters above the firmament. Consider also the following verses: "Can you, like him, spread out the skies, hard as a cast metal mirror?" (Job 37:18); "The One who builds His upper chambers in the heavens and has founded His vaulted dome over the earth" (Amos 9:6 NASB); and "When he made firm the skies above" (Proverbs 8:28). These are apt descriptions of how the sky looked to the ancient Hebrews. As Denis Lamoureux explains, "What did the divinely inspired author of Genesis 1 see when he looked up? A huge blue dome. To suggest that there was a sea of water in the heavens being held up by a solid structure was completely reasonable to him. Believing the sun, moon, and stars were placed in the firmament in front of the heavenly sea is exactly what it looks like from an ancient phenomenological perspective."[69] And indeed in Psalm 148:4 we read about the heavenly sea: "Praise him, you highest heavens, and you waters above the heavens!"

The biblical authors did understand that rain came from clouds. For example, in Judges 5:4 we read, "Lord, when you went out from Seir, when you marched from the region of Edom, the earth trembled and the heavens dropped, yes, the clouds dropped water." Also see 1 Kings 18:45, "And in a little while the heavens grew black with clouds and wind, and there was a great rain." And yet they also believed in windows in the firmament that opened to allow heavenly waters to fall to earth. Consider these passages from Job and Amos: "Have you entered the storehouses of the snow, or have you seen the storehouses of the hail?" (Job 38:22); "Who builds his upper chambers in the heavens and founds his vault upon the earth; who calls for the waters of the sea and pours them out upon the surface of the earth—the

Lord is his name" (Amos 9:6). Perhaps this was a source of scientific controversy in that day. Or perhaps the ancients believed that rain came from clouds, yet there also were retractable windows in the sky that could unleash the cosmic sea.

As for the waters below the earth, take a look at Exodus 20:4, part of the Ten Commandments: "You shall not make for yourself a carved image, or any likeness of anything that is in heaven above, or that is in the earth beneath, or that is in the water under the earth." This speaks not only to the oceans, but also to the waters "under" the earth. Likewise, David writes, "The earth is the Lord's and the fullness thereof, the world and those who dwell therein, for he has founded it upon the seas and established it upon the rivers" (Psalm 24:1–2). In Psalm 136:6, the psalmist writes "to him who spread out the earth above the waters." And lest we think this is just an Old Testament viewpoint, also note the NKJV translation of 2 Peter 3:5, "For this they willfully forget: that by the word of God the heavens were of old, and the earth standing out of water and in the water." Paul Seely concludes an article on ancient science thusly: "In summary, according to inspired comments on Gen 1:10, that is, Pss 24:2 and 136:6, the earth of Gen 1:10 was founded upon the sea, spread out upon the sea. The earth of Gen 1:10 is thus a flat earth-continent floating upon the sea. This is in perfect agreement with the historical definition."[70] Again, we see "agreement" between the Bible and historical science.

But what about the pillars? Wasn't the earth founded upon pillars, not water? Well, Kyle Greenwood explains that both possibilities had adherents in the ancient world: "Two main possibilities emerged. One solution was that the earth was supported by pillars. Another solution was that the earth actually floated on the waters."[71] And actually, it could have been both. In other words, many ancients believed there was some land below the earth, but also lots of water and pillars, such that "the terrestrial world was imagined as a great hollow structure resting on the 'deep.'"[72]

In addition to waters below the earth, ancient Hebrews also thought that there was a literal underworld. This is often called *Sheol* in the Bible and is a part of a three-tiered universe. This bottom level, writes Paul Seely, is where the souls of the departed live.[73] One of the places in the Bible where the underworld makes an appearance is in Numbers 16:33, where Korah, his 250 associate rebels, and all that belonged to them "went down alive into Sheol, and the earth closed over them, and they perished from the midst of the assembly." (I am not doubting the biblical story here. I believe that the ground opened up and swallowed 250 men. My point is that the Holy Spirit incorporated the readers' scientific understanding into the telling of the event). As Seely explains,

Not just the men, but their goods as well dropped down into the subterranean place. This is not figurative; men do not enter alive into a state of death; nor is it easy to say that material goods enter a state of death. ... It is not the state of death nor the grave that is in view in Numbers 16, but the subterranean realm of the dead. And the picture could scarcely be drawn more clearly. The floor of the middle story opened up, and the men standing on it fell down into the bottom story. They did not 'go down' figuratively, but literally."[74]

Isaiah 14:9 provides another example. "Sheol beneath is stirred up to meet you when you come; it rouses the shades to greet you, all who were leaders of the earth; it raises from their thrones all who were kings of the nations." *Shades* would seem to refer to those that have died and are awaiting the Day of Judgment. Another example is from the New Testament: "So that at the name of Jesus every knee should bow, in heaven and on earth and under the earth" (Philippians 2:10). Quite likely, "under the earth" refers to the bottom layer of the three-tiered universe.[75] In Ephesians 4:8–10, Paul may be speaking of Jesus descending into Sheol during the three days after his death to celebrate with believers who had died. Paul starts by quoting Psalm

68:18 and then explains that Jesus fulfilled that prophecy: "Therefore it says: 'When he ascended on high he led a host of captives, and he gave gifts to men.' (In saying, 'He ascended,' what does it mean but that he had also descended into the lower regions, the earth? He who descended is the one who also ascended far above the heavens, that he might fill all things.)" So we have the New Testament using a depiction of a physical place within the bowels of the earth, which everyone at the time believed in, to explain a spiritual realm.

We have also already seen flat earth and geocentric verses. Earlier, we quoted Psalm 104 and Ecclesiastes 1. There are plenty of other verses that show that the Holy Spirit employed this science of the day. For example, 1 Chronicles 16:30 reads, "Tremble before him, all the earth; yes, the world is established; it shall never be moved." Psalm 19:6, referring to the sun, proclaims, "Its rising is from the end of the heavens, and its circuit to the end of them, and there is nothing hidden from its heat." Psalm 75:3 states, "When the earth totters, and all its inhabitants, it is I who keep steady its pillars." All of this is in alignment with the ancients' scientific perspective. As Kyle Greenwood relates, "In both Egypt and Mesopotamia the earth was thought to be a flat disk. The horizon constituted the ends of the earth. Where the earth ended, the cosmic seas began. This is evident in both visual representations and textual descriptions. ... As with the Mesopotamians, the Egyptians' world revolved around them and extended radially until it reached the cosmic seas."[76] So I can surmise that the Holy Spirit was not teaching modern science because the authors were using the science of the time.

No Modern Science in the Bible, Part 3

The third reason why I believe that the Holy Spirit did not intend to teach modern science is easiest to express in the form of two rhetorical questions: If He intended to teach modern science, of what modern era? Are we a specially chosen generation?

Science is changing. It is a learning process, and we will continue to learn. Any science that the Holy Spirit chose to reveal in Scripture would have been either too advanced or not advanced enough for its readers, except in the case of one generation. As John Walton explains, "Another problem with concordism (the idea that biblical and scientific teaching ought to harmonize) is that it assumes that the text should be understood in reference to current scientific consensus, which would mean that it would neither correspond to last century's scientific consensus nor to that which may develop in the next century."[77] Also, John Lennox puts it well when he says, "If the biblical explanation were at the level, say, of twenty-second-century science, it would likely be unintelligible to everyone, including scientists today."[78]

The Holy Spirit had to choose the science of one era to speak in. The obvious choice was to use the science of the original audience. The Bible was, after all, written to an original audience. And although it was written for all of us, I believe God would be justified in expecting later generations, including ours, to understand what choice He made and why He made it, and to therefore recognize that the science in the Bible would not contradict the scientific presumptions of the original audience. Consider what would have happened if Jesus had used modern science in His discourses while He was on earth, rather than speaking to people using the science of the day. No one would have understood Him. At worst, everyone would have thought He was crazy and ignored Him. At best, a fascination with the "new science" would have been a major distraction from His message.

No Modern Science in the Bible, Part 4

Fourth, the Hebrews would not have understood the Big Bang. Why then would God tell them about it? Or as Francis Collins rhetorically asks, "Would it have served God's purposes thirty-four hundred years ago to lecture His people about radioactive decay, geologic strata, and

DNA?"[79] I also like this quote from Augustine: "One does not read in the Gospel that the Lord said: 'I will send you the Paraclete who will teach you about the course of the sun and moon.' For He willed to make them Christians, not mathematicians."[80]

The Bible Doesn't Teach Ancient Science

So the Holy Spirit did not teach the science of any time after (or before, obviously) the time period in which the books were written. It is likewise the case that the Holy Spirit did not intend to teach the science of the ancient Near East, home to the Bible's original audience. The argument in support of this proposition is concise and clear: The science of the ancient Near East was not true, and "it is impossible for God to lie" (Hebrews 6:18).[81] God would not have taught things that are not true. But was God being untruthful when He put the scientific language of the day in the Bible? Absolutely not! He was not teaching the science of the day as truth. When God used the science of the ancient Near East, He was accommodating, using concepts that His readers understood, to convey theological truth that the original audience could grasp.

As discussed earlier, God does this throughout the Bible. Indeed, God continues to accommodate each of us on a regular basis. Denis Lamoureux points out, "As Christians we experience divine accommodation personally in our prayer life. Does the Lord not descend to speak to you at your spiritual and intellectual level?"[82] Yes, He absolutely does. And it was true also with respect to the Hebrews; God adapted His communication to them in the context of their culture and base of knowledge. Therefore, we need to distinguish between what is part of the accommodation and what is affirmed and taught by Scripture. Inspiration attaches to the theological truth being claimed, not the science being incidentally used as an aid.

Conclusion: Genesis 1 Employs Figurative Language

If the Holy Spirit did not intend to teach modern science, and did not intend to teach the science of the time, then it must be the case that He did not intend to teach science at all. Science is just not the point. Which makes sense. As Bernard Ramm quips, "Christianity is a religion and not a science."[83] Likewise Praveen Sethupathy posits that "the Bible's primary objective is not to describe the mathematical language, physical law or chemical makeup of the world."[84]

Science is not the point. To ask another rhetorical question, why would God lead with a science lesson? The opening chapter of the Bible is extremely valuable real estate. In a sense, with the likely exception of the Gospels, the opening pages of Genesis constitute the most valuable real estate in the world. When a person picks up the Bible for the first time, they often go either to the Gospels or to Genesis 1. God could put anything He wanted at the beginning of the book of His Word. He could tell us about who He is, who we are, and what our relationship with Him is. And I believe He did exactly that. I do not think He meant to instead give us a science textbook.

Since science is not the point, we have no reason to expect that the creation account in Genesis 1 provides a scientifically accurate portrayal of creation. Indeed, we have every reason to expect that it does not. The Holy Spirit does not teach science. So the Holy Spirit is not trying to teach us how, scientifically, the universe, earth, plants, animals, and humans were created. Thus, we have every reason to conclude that Genesis 1 is not a literal account of creation.[85] If it is not a literal account, then it must be a figurative portrayal. In the following chapters, we will see that a figurative reading of Genesis 1 allows for a coherent interpretation.

Notes

64 John H. Walton in *Four Views on the Historical Adam*, eds. Matthew Barrett and Ardel B. Caneday (Grand Rapids, MI: Zondervan, 2013), 116–17.

65 Hugh Ross, *More than a Theory* (Grand Rapids, MI: Baker Books, 2009), 101.

66 Dennis Linscomb, "The Ancient Near Eastern Context of the Genesis Creation and Flood Stories and Its Impact on Biblical Inspiration," Academia, January 4, 2016, https://www.academia.edu/20019677/The_Ancient_Near_Eastern_Context_of_the_Genesis_Creation_and_Flood_Stories_and_Its_Impact_on_Biblical_Inspiration.

67 Kyle Greenwood, *Scripture and Cosmology* (Downers Grove, IL: Intervarsity, 2015), 69.

68 Arie Leegwater, "A Hard Lesson: Interpretation, Genomic Data, and the Scriptures," *Journal of the American Scientific Affiliation* 62, no. 3 (2010): 145–46.

69 Denis O. Lamoureux in *Four Views on the Historical Adam*, eds. Matthew Barrett and Ardel B. Caneday (Grand Rapids, MI: Zondervan, 2013), 51.

70 Paul H. Seely, "The Geographical Meaning of 'Earth' and 'Seas' in Genesis 1:10," *Westminster Theological Journal* 59 (1997): 231–55.

71 Greenwood, *Scripture and Cosmology*, 69.

72 Lewis Spence, *Myths & Legends of Babylonia & Assyria* (n.p.: Sagwan, 2018), 86.

73 Paul H. Seely, "The Three-Storied Universe," *The Journal of the American Scientific Affiliation* 21 (1969): 18–22.

74 Seely, 18–22.

75 Lamoureux, *Four Views*, 48.

76 Greenwood, *Scripture and Cosmology*, 41, 43.

77 John H. Walton, *The Lost World of Genesis One* (Downers Grove, IL: IVP Academic, 2009), 15.

78 John Lennox, *Seven Days that Divide the World* (Grand Rapids, MI: Zondervan 2011), 29–30.

79 Francis S. Collins, *The Language of God* (New York: Free Press, 2006), 175.

80 Augustine, *De actis contra Felicem Manichaeum*. Book I, Chapter X.

81 See also Numbers 23:19, "God is not a man, that he should lie, or a son of man, that he should change his mind."

82 Lamoureux, *Four Views*, 54.

83 Bernard Ramm, *The Christian View of Science and Scripture* (Grand Rapids, MI: Eerdmans, 1954), 245.

84   Praveen Sethupathy in *How I Changed My Mind About Evolution*, eds. Kathryn Applegate and J. B. Stump (Downers Grove, IL: IVP Academic, 2016), 106.

85   Here I am using the modern American meaning of "literal," which is, via Merriam-Webster, "according to the letter of the scriptures." Accessed September 6, 2019, https://www.merriam-webster.com/dictionary/literal.

CHAPTER 10

....

An Assist from Ancient Near Eastern Literature

Does a figurative reading detract from the truthfulness or sacredness of Scripture? Not at all. Just the opposite, actually. A literal reading restricts the meaning of Genesis, insomuch as it confines it to a scientific account. The use of figurative language allows for rich meaning through the use of symbolism. As Conrad Hyers puts it,

> *In the literal treatment of the six days of creation, a modern, arithmetical reading is substituted for the original, symbolic one. This results, unwittingly, in a secular rather than a religious interpretation. Not only are the symbolic associations and meanings of the text lost in the process, but the text is needlessly placed in conflict with scientific and historical readings of origins.*[86]

The use of figurative language adds depth to the text. It allows the author to convey deep theological truth.

Note that Hyers points out that the original meaning was a symbolic one, and I agree. But how do we access the meaning? How do we figure out what the author intended to convey? The answer is to understand the intentions and mindset of the author and the experiences, viewpoints, and attitudes of the readers he was addressing. It is about putting ourselves in the shoes of the author and of the audience. What was the author trying to do, and how was he going about it? What was the framework through which the audience was likely to access the message? In all of this, understanding context is critical.

This can be difficult even with regard to modern writing. I often have struggled to fully grasp what Bob Dylan is getting at in some of his songs. Several things are helpful, however. I am fluent in English, the language his songs are written in. Dylan is an American artist, and the songs have been written within my lifetime, or close to it (within about ten years); therefore, I have some understanding of the cultural and societal backdrop of the time when they were written. I also know about some of the contemporaneous events and experiences in Dylan's life and times that may have inspired and shaped his songs. I am pretty well versed in the musical environment of his time, and so I can assess how Dylan has been influenced by his peers, how he has conversed with them, and how he has influenced their music. In addition, I recognize and appreciate the full range of genres that Dylan employs in his writing—from folk to talking blues to surrealistic dreamscapes to gospel to poetry and more. These things help me in trying to access Dylan's intent and mindset, and they give me a framework, as part of his audience, for observing the intended meaning.

Accessing early Genesis can be much more difficult than interpreting Bob Dylan's music. I don't know ancient Hebrew at all. I am thousands of years and half a globe removed from the ancient Israelites. The culture and society of the ancient Israelites were markedly different from my own, to put it mildly. What then am I to do? The best way to understand the context of early Genesis is to become familiar with the times, culture, and cognitive environment of the Hebrews and their neighbors. One way to do this is to reach an understanding of the science of the day, as we have. Another way is to study other books in the Old Testament. We do some of that here in this book. But perhaps the best way to familiarize ourselves with the world of the ancient Hebrews is to explore the literature of the ancient Near East. In particular, it is helpful to explore ancient Near Eastern literature that touches on topics similar to those of Genesis 1–11.

Fortunately, archeologists have unearthed a plethora of literature from the ancient Near East. Importantly for our present purposes, we now have access to the creation and flood literature of surrounding cultures. This can give us a sense of context. It can help put us in the shoes of the author and of the audience.

The most influential piece of creation literature in the ancient Near East, by all accounts, was *Enuma Elish*. Parts of this grand Babylonian creation epic date back to at least 2500 BC and likely even earlier.[87] The opening lines read, "When above, were not raised the heavens: and below on earth a plant had not grown up; the abyss also had not broken open their boundaries: The chaos Tiamat was the producing-mother of the whole of them."[88] Tiamat, the god of fresh waters, is the mother who gives birth to all of the other gods. The father is the god of salt waters, Apsu. Tiamat and Apsu are annoyed by the racket coming from the minor gods, who do all the work. These minor gods are partying too hard—"So they proved bothersome to Tiamat, their hullabaloo echoed."[89] Apsu, against the objection of Tiamat, determines to kill all of the minor gods to stop the racket so that he and Tiamat might get some rest. Ea, one of the minor gods, gets wind of the plot and preemptively kills Apsu. Tiamat vows vengeance. She enlists the help of a few other major gods and gathers a demon army.

The minor gods catch wind of her plans. Marduk, at the time a minor god, rides out to pre-emptively attack her, and after an epic battle he slays Tiamat, cutting her in two.[90] Marduk uses Tiamat's entrails to make the heavens and the earth and then divides the upper from the lower waters and sets lights in the heaven. Marduk then decides to make humans, that the humans may perform the work of the gods for them and give the gods rest—"So thus I am well inclined to give rise to primal humanity. And the work which is now done by the gods, he will do, so that the gods will not be required to labor for evermore."[91] Marduk executes Kingu, one of the gods that aligned himself with Tiamat and who served as the leader of her armies, and then Marduk uses Kingu's blood to make mankind. Marduk becomes king of the pantheon.[92]

Atrahasis is another famous ancient Near Eastern story, and it features a giant flood. We will look in more detail at the flood portion of this story in a later chapter, but for now it is worth noting that near the beginning of the tale, the gods create humans to do their work for them. As Copan and Jacoby relate,

The junior-level gods rebel after becoming frustrated with the work of digging canals, and a war between the gods ensues. Now the gods are no longer willing to carry out their backbreaking work. What to do? The problem is solved by the creation of humans. Seven original males and females are made from dust combined with the blood of a sacrificed god. The humans' purpose? To take over the menial labors of the gods so that they may no longer be fatigued, but content.[93]

There are several Egyptian creation accounts as well. As David Leeming writes, "In spite of constant development over the centuries, certain aspects of an Egyptian creation myth can be said to be relatively constant. These include a source of all things in the primeval waters."[94] One prominent tradition from the Pyramid Texts was that the creator god Atum emerged from these waters through an act of self-creation and proceeded to create the other gods. As Kenton Sparks relates, Atum accomplished this by standing upon a mound that emerged from the primeval waters, sneezing out the gods of air and moisture and then continuing with other acts of creation.[95]

There are many other creation myths from the region. Tremper Longman discusses a Canaanite creation myth[96] in which Yam, whose name means "sea," leads a coup against the creator god Baal (whom many apostate Israelites worshipped). The *Sumerian King List* is another important work of literature from the ancient Near East. The list provides parenthetical details of each king's reign, thus describing a primeval history that culminated in a great flood, followed by an ancient historical record that ends at approximately 2000 BC. The lifespans of the pre-flood Sumerian kings are extraordinarily long, just as we see in the Genesis account. The oldest versions of the *King List* are old indeed, far older than Genesis. Yet another creation myth is the Sumerian *Enki and Ninmah*, which "depicts mankind created of clay, also for the purpose of relieving the gods from their hard duties."[97]

What can we say about these creation accounts? These are epic tales, sagas, myths. They are not true in their details and are certainly not scientific narratives. It is unclear whether the pagan audiences of these stories viewed them as literal or figurative accounts. Either way, the stories were believed by their readers to convey deep truths about origins and other important matters. These types of accounts, these myths, were how deep truths were conveyed in the culture of the ancient Near East.

So this is what the Hebrews would have expected—their own grand, majestic epic, but one that was imbued with ultimate truth. This is the genre in which creation and flood stories were told. This is the medium that would have had the most impact on the Hebrews. As John Walton notes, "We expect Genesis to be characterized in part by the perspectives that are found in the literature of the ancient Near East because God was communicating into an ancient Near Eastern culture: ancient Israel."[98] And it appears, indeed, that that is what the Israelites got. God appears to have accommodated to the Israelites by giving early Genesis a similar shape to that of the surrounding creation and flood literature. As Vern Poythress puts it, "Genesis 1 is providing for the Israelites an alternative to the myths within their environment."[99]

It is worth pointing out, parenthetically, that the Hebrews had the perfect writer for such a text. Moses was the adopted grandson of the Pharaoh. He was raised and educated for 40 years in Pharaoh's court, where he would have been exposed to the literature of the ancient Near East, and where he would have learned how to craft a masterpiece of literature like Genesis. God furnished His appointed writer of Genesis with unique tools for the task.[100]

The similarities between, for example, *Enuma Elish* and Genesis 1 are too stark to ignore. Some can be seen simply from my terse summary of *Enuma Elish* above: for instance, the central role of the taming of the cosmic waters in creation. Creation in *Enuma Elish* arises out of the gods of the cosmic waters, represented by Tiamat and Apsu. Compare with Genesis 1:2, where "the Spirit of God was hovering over the face of the waters." In *Enuma Elish*, Marduk creates the world by cutting the water goddess Tiamat in two, with one half making the heavens and the other half forming the earth. Compare with Genesis 1:7, where God "made the expanse and separated the waters that were under the expanse from the waters that were above the expanse." Other similarities are only noticeable by reading the full story. For example, both texts invoke a divine assembly.[101] Light is absent at the beginning of each story, and when light appears it does so before the appearance of the sun or moon. Also, the order of creation is similar in both stories, and both conclude with divine rest. In the words of Claus Westermann, "There is a correspondence in the general succession of events: Chaos as the beginning, the creation of the firmament, of the dry land, of the heavenly bodies and of people. God's rest corresponds to the feast of the gods."[102] There are numerous other similarities as well.

There are so many similarities that when *Enuma Elish* was unearthed about 150 years ago, many scholars hypothesized that Genesis 1 was a simple retelling of *Enuma Elish* (which is older than Genesis). But such knee-jerk thinking hasn't persisted into the 21st century. We can easily see that Genesis is trying to tell a fundamentally different story and deliver a different message than *Enuma Elish*. It is clear, rather, that Genesis and *Enuma Elish* employ similar concepts and devices, which makes sense as both works of literature came from the same cultural environment. Israel was not an isolated island. They were a nation with many neighbors, a part of the Near East. Learned Hebrews would have read stories such as *Enuma Elish* directly. Unlearned Hebrews would likely have been exposed to the stories via travelling storytellers. Even Hebrews who had not been exposed to the written texts or the oral tradition would have picked up on the themes just from the diffusion of the stories into the cultural environment. Gordon Wenham makes a good analogy: A story like *Enuma Elish* was, in ancient times, similar to what Darwin's *On the Origin of Species* is today. Not many have actually read it, but almost everyone knows about it and understands the general message.[103]

It is also clear that Genesis 1 was in conversation with *Enuma Elish*, as Genesis contains different and often opposing perspectives on key themes. The author of Genesis seems to have used a well-known piece of literature in order to present Israel's own perspective. The similarities between the ancient Near Eastern creation accounts and Genesis serve to anchor the Genesis story in the Hebrews' cognitive environment, thereby making the stories and their lessons accessible. It is in the differences, of which there are many, that we look for the inspired meaning. What I have come to believe, along with many scholars, is that Genesis 1 is the Hebrew version of the traditional ancient Near Eastern creation account. God chose a format that His original audience was familiar with and understood, and used the differences to highlight deep theological truths. Genesis refers to some of the same events that the pagan myths cover, but "turns [the pagan myths] on their heads."[104] Genesis 1 gives a full-throated rejection of the religions and theologies of the surrounding cultures. In other words, Genesis 1 says: *This is what your neighbors say. Whether you've read it or not, you've heard it. And you've seen their religious practices. What you've read, heard, and seen is false. Here, now, is the truth.*

Notes

86 Conrad Hyers, *The Meaning of Creation* (Atlanta: John Knox, 1984), 75.

87 David Leeming, *A Dictionary of Creation Myths* (Oxford: Oxford University Press, 1995), 23.

88 See William Ryan and Walter Pitman, *Noah's Flood* (New York: Simon & Schuster Paperbacks, 1998), 50.

89 Timothy J. Stephany, *Enuma Elish* (United States: Createspace, 2014), 4.

90 Lewis Spence, *Myths & Legends of Babylonia & Assyria* (n.p.: Sagwan, 2018), 79.

91 Stephany, *Enuma Elish*, 38.

92 Alexander Heidel, *The Babylonian Genesis* (Chicago: The University of Chicago Press, 1963), 3–10.

93 Paul Copan and Douglas Jacoby, *Origins* (Nashville: Morgan James, 2019), 20.

94 David Leeming, *A Dictionary of Creation Myths*, 82.

95 Kenton L. Sparks, *Ancient Texts for the Study of the Hebrew Bible* (Grand Rapids, MI: Baker Academic, 2005), 323.

96 Tremper Longman III, *Genesis*, The Story of God Bible Commentary, eds. Tremper Longman III and Scot McKnight (Grand Rapids, MI: Zondervan, 2016), 30.

97 Kenneth A. Mathews, *Genesis 1–11:26*, The New American Commentary (Nashville: B&H, 1996), 95.

98 John H. Walton, *The Lost World of Adam and Eve* (Downers Grove, IL: IVP Academic, 2015), 198.

99 Vern S. Poythress, *Interpreting Eden* (Wheaton, IL: Crossway, 2019), 166.

100 I see no need to delve into the controversies surrounding the composition of Genesis. I presume that, at the very least, later editors were working off source material produced by Moses.

101 As I explain later, I believe the divine assembly in Genesis refers to the Trinity.

102 Claus Westermann, *Genesis 1-11* (Minneapolis: Fortress, 1994), 89.

103 Gordon Wenham, "The Perplexing Pentateuch," *Vox Evangelica* 17 (1987): 7–22.

104 Copan and Jacoby, *Origins*, 14.

CHAPTER 11

···

An Interpretation—
Introduction

But what is that truth? Now that we have accessed the cognitive environment of the authors and the audience, what are the intentions of the author? What are the lessons? Well, early Genesis is the trailhead of the entire Bible. As such, while we should in one sense let the Genesis 1 text speak for itself, we should also be on the lookout for messages that set up the grand themes of the rest of the Bible; this is just good exegesis, reading Genesis in the context of the Bible as a whole. Among other things, we should expect to see lessons about God's attributes—such as His sovereignty, power, glory, holiness, loyalty, and love. We should expect to learn about the purpose of creation and our role in the world—that we are made to reflect God's glory and to worship Him in eternity. We should anticipate that the text will set the table for teaching us about Jesus.

The Days

As we delve into the meanings of Genesis 1, and before we proceed with a verse-by-verse, day-by-day analysis, let's start with the structure of the account. What about those days? Ah yes, the days. To appreciate the reasons for the use of this literary device, we need to start with an appreciation of the sophistication and richness of the text. It turns out that there are multiple good hypotheses as to why the author employed the device of the days, and more than one can be true at the same time.

One explanation that is compelling to me is the portrayal of the universe as God's temple, which is constructed over six days and occupied on the seventh day. According to Gordon Wenham, "The pattern of six days of similar acts followed by a change on the seventh day is well attested in Mesopotamian and Ugaritic literature."[105] In particular, it is common with regard to temple construction. The ancient Near Eastern literature is replete with accounts of temple construction and dedication. In these accounts, the construction of the temple is followed by a dedication ceremony. This dedication ceremony often lasts for seven days. On the seventh day, the deity enters the temple and rests in it, taking up residence and ruling his domain from the temple. Iain Provan emphasizes "the close connection between temple and cosmos in the ancient mind and the marked similarity between ancient Near Eastern texts concerning the making of the world and those concerning the construction of temples."[106] On one level of meaning, then, Genesis 1 describes the creation of God's temple, the universe. It is created in six days, and then on the seventh day it is finished and God takes up residence in it, resting in and ruling over the universe. As John Walton explains, in the ancient world the temple was not just the deity's home, it was "more importantly his headquarters—the control room. When the deity rests in the temple it means that he is taking command."[107] The original audience would have recognized the parallels and understood that Genesis 1 was talking about temple construction.

Note that in this perspective, the separation of creation into days does more than provide underlying structure to the narrative. It also provides meaning. Among other things, the construction of a cosmic temple states that the whole universe is God's temple, such that God is the Lord of the entire universe. Also, the universe is sacred space, and we must treat it as such.

Creation concludes with a period of rest. But in the ancient Near East, rest does not mean leisure. Rest means order and rule. To again quote Walton, "God has ordered the cosmos with the purpose of taking up his residence in it and ruling over it. Day seven is the reason for days one through six. It is the fulfillment of God's purpose."[108] God's work of salvation and of ruling the world are not "work" to Him in a pejorative sense: this is not difficult and profitless labor. Reigning in majesty, with both perfect love and perfect justice, is an expression of who He is. For God, sitting on His throne is resting.

A second reason for the literary device of the seven days may be to portray God's creative work within another structure that the audience would have well understood—that of a workweek followed by a well-deserved day off. As John Collins remarks, "The structure of the account shows us that our author has presented God as if he were a craftsman going about his workweek."[109] This anchors the story in a structure that is easily grasped and identified with, allowing the reader or hearer to focus on the details and messages. And here again, the structure provides force and clarity to a key message of the text: the importance and sanctity of the Sabbath.

Another explanation of the days has to do with what is commonly referred to as the Framework Theory. This theory goes back at least as far as Johann Gottfried Herder (1744–1803), a poet (among other things) who saw poetical elements in the arrangement of Genesis 1. The theory has many modern-day proponents and hinges on the parallelism of days one, two, and three with days four, five, and six. Day one and day four concern the heavens. Days two and five deal with the sea and the air. Days three and six deal with land. Furthermore, there is a distinct pattern whereby in days one, two, and three, realms are created, while in days four, five, and six, those realms are filled. Herder recognized "the parallelism of the heavens and the earth" in the Genesis 1 text, and that creation was "separated and classed in order."[110] So in day one God creates the heavens, and in day four He fills the heavens with the sun, moon, and stars. In day two God creates the seas and the air, and in day five He fills them both with creatures. In day three God creates land, and in day six He fills the land with animals and with humans.

At least two things are worth highlighting regarding the Framework Theory. First, in the parallelism we see the fulfillment of the promise of verse 2. In verse 2 the earth was "formless and void." So in the first three days, God provides form by creating realms. In days four through six, God tackles the "void" part, making full the empty realms. Second, the numbers involved are highly symbolic. Three was an auspicious number in ancient Near Eastern thought, and it has special significance in the Bible as well. Two sets of three days add up to six, and adding the day of rest makes seven. Seven "has the numerological meaning of wholeness, plenitude, and completeness" in the ancient Near East.[111]

Notes

105   Gordon J. Wenham, *Genesis 1–15*, World Bible Commentary (Grand Rapids, MI: Zondervan, 1987), 19.

106   Iain Provan, *Seriously Dangerous Religion* (Waco, TX: Baylor University Press, 2014), 59–60.

107   John H. Walton, *The Lost World of Genesis One* (Downers Grove, IL: IVP Academic, 2009), 74.

108   John H. Walton, *The Lost World of Adam and Eve* (Downers Grove, IL: IVP Academic, 2015), 49.

109   C. John Collins, *Genesis 1–4* (Phillipsburg, NJ: P&R, 2006), 77.

110   Johann Gottfried Herder, *The Spirit of Hebrew Poetry* (Forgotten Books, 2012), 1:58.

111   Conrad Hyers, *The Meaning of Creation* (Atlanta: John Knox, 1984), 76.

CHAPTER 12

Verse 1

So now we're finally ready to take a detailed look at Genesis 1. Let's comb through it one verse or day at a time. As we'll see, it serves as a de facto national anthem for the Israelites and introduces several crucial theological themes. Verse 1 reads:

In the beginning, God created the heavens and the earth.

As we touched on earlier, there are multiple views as to the purpose of this verse. Let's look at two minor views and then at the two reigning major viewpoints.

One minority viewpoint is called the "gap theory." In this view, the world is created in its entirety and in perfection in verse 1. Then there is a gap of an indeterminate amount of time between verse 1 and verse 2. In that gap of time, things go wrong. Satan rebels, and God destroys the world. Verse 2 shows the dark and chaotic state of the world after Satan's rebellion. Out of this chaos God remakes the world as described by the rest of the passage. This view was popular in the early 1900s. It has since fallen out of favor, although it still has adherents. The adherents, I think, seem to be reading an awful lot into the text.

Another minor view, but one which I think is quite credible, is that verses 1 and 2 should be translated, "In the beginning when God

created the heavens and the earth, the earth was formless and void..."
This closely matches the opening of *Enuma Elish* ("When the heavens
above had not been named") as well as the second creation account
at Genesis 2:4b ("in the day that the Lord God made the earth and
the heavens"). There are grammatical arguments for and against this
view.[112] Overall, while some popular translations such as the NRSV
use this phrasing, the weight of the evidence appears to be against
it. One noteworthy implication of this translation is that the verse
does not provide evidence for ex-nihilo creation, as instead it paints
a picture of God making or forming out of pre-existing materials.
However, even if ex-nihilo creation is not established in verse 1, it is
well established in the New Testament. Finally, note that this rendering
causes verse 1 to serve as an introduction of the creation account, if
not a summary per se.

Now we can address the two main viewpoints. The traditional
view is that verse 1 records the first creation event. Whatever is present
in verse 2 was created in verse 1. Historically this was the majority
viewpoint, and this traditional authority is a key selling point to the
adherents of this view. They believe that Genesis 1:1–2 ought to be
understood to mean—and worded to say—that a creation act (verse
1) resulted in an earth that was in the state of being formless and
void (verse 2). Despite its historical prevalence, this has become the
minority opinion among biblical researchers, though several eminent
scholars do continue to hold to it. A good case for this viewpoint is
given by Vern Poythress.[113]

The second main viewpoint, and the one that I hold to, is that
verse 1 is a summary of the chapter that follows. In modern times
this has become the majority viewpoint in scholarly circles.[114] To my
mind, verse 1 reads naturally as an introduction, especially as "the
heavens and the earth" seems to indicate a full, completed universe.[115]
Further, I think that verse 1 serves as the front of a bookend with
Genesis 2:1–3. Verse 1 introduces the creation account to follow, and
Genesis 2:1–3 announces its completion. The order of *God, created,*

and *the heavens and the earth* in verse 1 are reversed in Genesis 2:1–3. Also, Genesis 1:1 and 2:1–3 each have, in the Hebrew, a multiple of seven words. Furthermore, if verse 1 is viewed as a framing device in the vein of the toledots, it would make Genesis 2:1–3 the first of twelve narrative sections. As twelve is a symbolic biblical number, this makes more sense than having eleven.[116] Furthermore, I am swayed by the fact that verse 1 doesn't give detail on what parts of the heaven and earth were created. Perhaps it should be inferred from what we see as existing in verse 2, but that seems a bit tortured to me. The remainder of Genesis 1 announces the creation of everything else in some detail, so why just leave it to us in verse 1 to infer the creation of the primal waters and the earth's core? Also, God introduces the rest of His created acts with the phrase "And God said," which is missing from verse 1. Finally, viewing verse 1 as an introduction makes more sense when Genesis 1 is seen from a figurative perspective.

Verse 1, as a summary, is to be taken literally. God did, literally, create the heavens and the earth. The rest of the chapter explains that creation using figurative language. So verse 1 is saying, "This is what I will be, in figurative language, explaining." This is similar in some respects to Matthew 13. In that chapter, Jesus introduces each of seven parables with the phrase, "The kingdom of heaven is like..." Now, there is a literal kingdom of heaven, but what follows in each of the parables is figurative language. I see the same type of setup here. The figurative language of the rest of Genesis 1 is relating to something real. Genesis 1 as a whole is explaining the literal truth of its first verse.

For such a seemingly simple and literal sentence, however, we are left with at least three questions. First, in the beginning of what? The beginning of time, or the beginning of the creation of the heavens and the earth? Second, do "the heavens and the earth" incorporate the whole universe, or just the earth and the sky? Third, did God create out of existing materials or ex-nihilo? The answers may seem self-evident, but from the text they are actually not.

I take "In the beginning" to mean the beginning of time, space, matter, and energy, such that there was nothing created before verse 1. On this point the text is a little vague. It could be argued that the beginning refers to the beginning of God's creative work, which could have employed materials that always existed, but the context seems to point to the beginning of time and space. As Gordon Wenham comments, "The context here [1:1] and in Gen 1 suggest [beginning] refers to the beginning of time itself, not to a particular period within eternity."[117]

As for what God created, I hold that He created everything. That is, "the heavens and the earth" includes the universe and everything in it. If, as I propose, "In the beginning" refers to the beginning of time and space, then God created it all, as there was nothing before the beginning, and He created all after that beginning. In addition, the Hebrew supports this view. As *Nelson's NKJV Study Bible* comments, "The heavens and the earth mean 'all of creation' or 'the cosmos.'"[118] Furthermore, there is scriptural support from the New Testament. John 1:3 states, "All things were made through him, and without him was not any thing made that was made." Colossians 1:16–17 declares, "For by him all things were created, in heaven and on earth, visible and invisible. … And he is before all things, and in him all things hold together." Finally, Revelation 4:11 says, "For you created all things, and by your will they existed and were created."

What did God create out of? Pre-existing material or out of nothing? The exact wording of the Hebrew text is noncommittal here. Some commentators believe that *bara*, the word used for "create" (other Hebrew words could have been used for "create"), is only used to denote ex-nihilo creation, but others disagree. However, as He created at the beginning of time and space, there was nothing to create out of except what He Himself created. Also, the fact that the text does not mention what God created everything out of is a hint that He created ex-nihilo. In addition, Hebrews 11:3 tells us that "what is seen was not made out of things that are visible." So God, at the beginning of space and time, created the universe out of nothing.

Now that we have a handle on what the text is saying, we can delve into the meaning. The primary lesson of Genesis 1 is that there is only one God. This may not seem like a big deal to us, but back in biblical times it was revolutionary. The Hebrews were surrounded by cultures that worshipped many gods. So the Bible is saying that all of the other gods are frauds. As Scot McKnight puts it, "All of the gods of the ancient Near East are eliminated in the theology of Genesis 1, and one supreme God, YHWH, is left standing."[119] This lesson was so important for God to get across to the Israelites that He made sure they couldn't miss it. It is right smack in the middle of verse 1 and is highlighted again and again throughout the first few books of the Bible; the first commandment offers a notable example. If God puts a piece of information in the first verse of His Word and also in His first commandment, you better pay attention. It's as if He is hitting the Israelites over the head with a stone tablet. Which is basically what happened. Recall how in Exodus 32 Moses descended Mount Sinai with the Ten Commandments in hand, only to observe the Israelites worshipping a golden calf; he threw the stone tablets down in righteous anger and despair, whereupon they broke. God certainly needed to be emphatic, as the Hebrews had constant struggles with worshipping other gods.

Another lesson is that there is a beginning to everything. Again, this may not seem like a big insight to us. We have dated the age of the earth, and modern cosmology teaches that, via the Big Bang, the universe had a beginning. But in ancient times this was not understood. The lack of a beginning was prominent in ancient Near Eastern thought. As Kenneth Mathews explains, "The cosmogonic stories told little about creation itself but focused on theogony (origins of the gods). The gods of creation were depicted primarily as re-ordering unruly primeval matter, not creating matter."[120] For example, the Egyptian creation accounts had gods emerging from pre-existing materials. Also, in *Enuma Elish* and other Babylonian and Sumerian creation accounts, the stories begin with the gods just being there. "For the Babylonians matter was eternal."[121] In contrast, in Genesis the universe was created out of nothing—ex-nihilo. This is a significant difference from rival creation accounts.

God is also taking credit for the creation of the universe. He was not created within the universe. He exists eternally, before the universe and outside of the universe, and is sovereign over creation. This lesson is echoed in Psalm 90:2, which proclaims, "Before the mountains were brought forth, or ever you had formed the earth and the world, from everlasting to everlasting you are God." Also, as we are told in 1 Peter 1:20, "He was foreknown before the foundation of the world." The gods of the ancient Near East were different. As Iain Provan explains, "The gods of the ancient Near East are certainly not sovereign over creation. They do not even truly create at all. Rather, they find themselves in a cosmos that has already emerged, and whose basic characteristics have already been laid down as the gods themselves are coming into existence."[122]

As God exists outside of time, He can see into the past and the future. This has a profound implication for His relationship with believers: He has known and loved each one of us, individually, since before time began. His love for us is eternal. As Ephesians 1:4–5 says, "He chose us in him before the foundation of the world, that we should be holy and blameless before him. In love he predestined us for adoption to himself as sons through Jesus Christ, according to the purpose of his will." How awesome that the Creator of the universe loves us with a love that is eternal!

I'll make one more point before we turn our attention to verse 2. Verse 1 showcases the immense, unfathomable power and glory of God. Indeed, "the first sentence itself is really a cry of praise."[123] Step back a moment and try to consider what is required to create the universe. We have a God whose might is so great that it is beyond our ability to comprehend. This should fill us with awe, respect, and reverence for our almighty Lord and Creator. That awe should lead to humility. As the psalmist says, "What is man that you are mindful of him, and the son of man that you care for him?" (Psalm 8:4). And humility should produce thanksgiving. For who are we? And "Yet you have made him a little lower than the heavenly beings and crowned him with glory and honor" (Psalm 8:5). This thankfulness should fill us with confidence. God can do all things. As Jeremiah exclaims, "Ah, Lord God! It is you who have made the heavens and the earth by your great power and by your outstretched arm! Nothing is too hard for you" (Jeremiah 32:17). This applies to God's actions in the world, such as raising His Son from the dead, and in our personal prayer life to the extent our prayers are in accord with His will.

Notes

112 Grammatical arguments against this rendering are given by Jeremy D. Lyon in "Genesis 1:1–3 and the Literary Boundary of Day One," *Journal of the Evangelical Theological Society* 62, no. 2 (2019): 269–85.

113 Vern S. Poythress, "Genesis 1:1 is the First Event, Not a Summary," *Westminster Theological Journal* 79 (2017): 97–121.

114 Gordon J. Wenham, *Genesis 1–15*, World Biblical Commentary (Grand Rapids, MI: Zondervan, 1987), 12.

115 Many Hebrew scholars agree. See Bruce K. Waltke, *Genesis* (Grand Rapids, MI: Zondervan, 2001), 59.

116 As mentioned earlier, this also takes 36:9 as a separate toledot rather than merely a repetition of 36:1. Many commentators hold that there are ten toledots in Genesis.

117 Gordon J. Wenham, *Genesis 1–15*, 14.

118 *Nelson's NKJV Study Bible* (Nashville: Thomas Nelson, 1999), 4.

119 Dennis R. Venema and Scot McKnight, *Adam and the Genome* (Grand Rapids, MI: Brazos, 2017), 119.

120 Kenneth A. Mathews, *Genesis 1–11:26*, The New American Commentary (Nashville: B&H, 1996), 117.

121 Alexander Heidel, *The Babylonian Genesis* (Chicago: The University of Chicago Press, 1963), 89.

122 Iain Provan, *Seriously Dangerous Religion* (Waco, TX: Baylor University Press, 2014), 54.

123 Claus Westermann, *Genesis 1–11* (Minneapolis: Fortress, 1994), 94.

CHAPTER 13

....

Verse 2

The earth was without form and void, and darkness was over the face of the deep. And the Spirit of God was hovering over the face of the waters.

We need to start our discussion of verse 2 with its relationship to verse 1. As mentioned earlier, one argument against the claim that verse 1 is an account of the first creative act is the question of what was created. If some things were created within the space of verse 1 and others were not, then we would expect the verse to explicitly say as much. So it seems that either everything was created in this specified moment or nothing was created, and thus if Genesis 1:1 is an account of an isolated creative act, then it ought to include everything that was created. But such an interpretation then causes much of Genesis 1:3–31 to make no sense, as it records the creation of many things. The other option, which I favor, is that nothing was created in verse 1—it is an introduction. In that case, however, verse 2 seems to make no sense, because in verse 2 some stuff already exists! This would seem to imply that God created using pre-existing materials, but we established above that God created ex-nihilo. So what is going on? There are two keys to the answer. One is that we won't be able to solve this puzzle using a literal mindset. The second is that Genesis 1 is not only concerned with material creation. It is also concerned with functional creation—it speaks, in good measure, of God creating order out of disorder and providing functions for things. A picture given in Genesis 1 is that of God forming His creation. Verse 2 highlights the initial materials with which God chose to work. God created these materials, and He also then used them. Of course, this is just a picture. We can learn about God's actual creation of the heavens and earth from the natural sciences.

Verse 2 is the beginning of the figurative portrayal of the creation. It starts with a scene that we will see is a very appropriate place to begin: the deep. The Israelite audience would have expected this, as in ancient Near East literature, creation springs from primeval waters. As Dennis Linscomb summarizes, "The author of Genesis wanted to account for the chaotic water because all of the ANE creation stories started with it, and it was part of the shared ANE cognitive framework."[124] With respect to Egyptian creation myths, specifically, Gordon Johnston explains that "the Hebrew depiction of the pre-creation state of the cosmos seems to echo the Egyptian idea of original infinite nothingness, an undifferentiated Monad—the infinite, static, lifeless, dark primordial sea."[125] Lewis Spence relates that in the Babylonian myths, "naught existed save the primeval ocean, [Tiamat], from whose fertile depths came every living thing."[126]

The deep, or the primeval waters, is a symbol and a source of chaos and disorder in the ancient Near East. In Genesis, God tames the deep (*tehom* in Hebrew), which is reminiscent of Marduk slaying Tiamat. Both tehom and Tiamat share the same root. If, as Peter Enns suggests, the play on words was intentional—"Slaying Tiamat is dimly reflected in God's taming the deep"[127]—that even further emphasizes the intentional differences between the ancient Near East accounts and Genesis. In the ancient Near East, conflict was involved in the creation of the earth out of primeval waters. In Genesis, there is no conflict. God has it all under control. He has quieted the seas, akin to when Jesus calmed the sea: "Then he rose and rebuked the winds and the sea, and there was a great calm" (Matthew 8:26). Another key difference is that in the ancient Near East, the deep is associated with gods. As Clarke Morledge writes, "Ancient pagan understandings of God viewed the 'deep waters' as either some type of god or some other rival to the authority of the gods. This is not so with Genesis. Genesis teaches us that the 'deep waters' stand subject to the work of God as the un-Rivaled and Ruling Creator."[128] In Genesis, as opposed to rival accounts, the primeval waters are just another creation of God. God reigns over the deep.

Verse 2 also introduces the Holy Spirit, saying, "The Spirit of God was hovering over the face of the waters." So we learn that the Holy Spirit participated in creation. Some will say that it is a mistake to see the Holy Spirit in the Old Testament, arguing that all doctrine relating to the Holy Spirit is based on the New Testament. But the Holy Spirit clearly makes many appearances in the Old Testament beyond Genesis 1:2. I'll give just a few examples.[129] There is Isaiah 42:1, where the Lord says of Jesus, "I have put my Spirit upon him; he will bring forth justice to the nations." The Holy Spirit is said to have come upon Samson: "And the Spirit of the LORD began to stir in him in Mahaneh-dan, between Zorah and Eshtaol" (Judges 13:25). And when Samuel anointed David king, "the Spirit of the LORD rushed upon David from that day forward" (1 Samuel 16:13). The Holy Spirit indwelt the prophets, which makes sense as their words, when written down, became Scripture, and all Scripture is inspired by the Holy Spirit. Ezekiel here describes his experience of being called by the Lord: "And as he spoke to me, the Spirit entered into me and set me on my feet, and I heard him speaking to me" (Ezekiel 2:2). So the Holy Spirit is all over the Old Testament and is first introduced in Genesis 1:2.

The text also produces a sense of anticipation, as the Spirit of God is hovering, preparing to work. Which leads us right into day one.

Notes

124 Dennis Linscomb, "The Ancient Near Eastern Context of the Genesis Creation and Flood Stories and Its Impact on Biblical Inspiration," Academia, January 4, 2016, https://www.academia.edu/20019677/The_Ancient_Near_Eastern_Context_of_the_Genesis_Creation_and_Flood_Stories_and_Its_Impact_on_Biblical_Inspiration.

125 Gordon H. Johnston, "Genesis 1 and Ancient Egyptian Creation Myths," *Bibliotheca Sacra* 165 (2008): 178–94.

126 Lewis Spence, *Myths & Legends of Babylonia & Assyria* (n.p.: Sagwan, 2018), 71.

127 Peter Enns, *The Evolution of Adam* (Grand Rapids, MI: Brazos, 2012), 40.

128 Clarke Morledge, "On the Use of Metaphor in Genesis One," Veracity, June 19, 2015, https://sharedveracity.net/2015/06/19/on-the-use-of-metaphor-in-genesis-one.

129 For discussion see, for example, https://www.thomasnelsonbibles.com/the-holy-spirit-in-the-old-testament, accessed September 13, 2019.

CHAPTER 14

Verse 3

And God said, "Let there be light," and there was light.

"And God said." The first thing to notice here is that when God spoke a command, the natural world changed accordingly. The Lord is effectual. He accomplishes what He sets out to do. He has power. To the original audience, this was likely anthropomorphism, with the picture being God the workman going about His work of creation, using His inner essence to make the earth.

This pattern—God speaks and then makes good on His Word—is repeated throughout Genesis 1. The accumulated effect of the pattern is to show us that God can be trusted. He is loyal.

From the New Testament, we see that there is also a deeper meaning. In John's Gospel, he testifies, "And the Word became flesh and dwelt among us" (1:14). God's Word is Jesus. And the world was created through Jesus, the Word: "All things were made through him, and without him was not anything made that was made" (John 1:3). Hebrews 1:2 concurs, "He has spoken to us by his Son … through whom also he created the world."

So we see that in each of the first three verses of the Bible, a member of the Trinity is introduced. God the Father in verse 1, the Holy Spirit in verse 2, and Jesus the Son in verse 3. The Bible opens by introducing us to God in the fullness and completeness of the Trinity. And each member of the Trinity plays a role in creation. So not only are Jesus and the Holy Spirit present along with the Father throughout the Old Testament, they are exalted along with the Father at the very fountainhead of the Bible.

"Let there be light." To the original audience, what was this light? On a literal level it was just that: light. The appearance of light before the creation of the sun would not have surprised them, as the same thing occurred in *Enuma Elish*. On a slightly deeper level, I hold this to be God unleashing His creative powers—dropping the curtains, so to speak, on His play of Creation. I imagine triumphant horns announcing the event. On a still deeper level, more accessible since the New Testament, light is a metaphor expressing God's goodness and truth: "God is light, and in him is no darkness at all" (1 John 1:5). Even deeper still, hinging on the use of light as the first act of creation, I believe that the text is telling us that creation is an outpouring of God's goodness. God's creation of life is a reflection and a manifestation of His vibrant love and a way for Him to express that love to us. As the apostle says in John 1:4–5, "In him was life, and the life was the light of men. The light shines in the darkness."

There is yet one more level of meaning we can access from this verse, and it is the deepest level of all. Paul likens the activity of the Holy Spirit in a believer's heart to the effect of light in Genesis 1:3. Paul writes, "For God, who said, 'Let light shine out of darkness,' has shone in our hearts to give the light of the knowledge of the glory of God in the face of Jesus Christ" (2 Corinthians 4:6). Charles Spurgeon makes use of this analogy and compares the entrance of light into the world in verse 3 to the entrance of the Holy Spirit into a believer's heart at the moment they are saved. In an 1875 sermon[130] he reflects that "the first day of creation fairly pictures the commencement of our spiritual life, our conviction, conversion, and first faith in Jesus." He goes on to add that, like the entrance of light in verse 3 after the preparation in verse 2, "the operations of grace are gradual, but its entrance is instantaneous."

In an earlier sermon[131] Spurgeon develops well this analogy, although without referring explicitly to 2 Corinthians 4:6. He explains that the "state of every human heart till God the Holy Spirit visits it" is akin to the earth in verse 2, formless and void. As in verse 2, with the Spirit of God hovering over the waters, "the secret work of the Holy Spirit begins in the human heart—we cannot always say precisely when or how." And the fruit of its "mysterious" works is to excite, "unsolicited" by us, "emotions, longings, desires" for God. And when the light comes, it shows us that without God we are lost. While there was darkness, "we think that we are righteous, that all is well with our souls; but when divine light comes in, we discover that we are fallen in Adam, and are terribly undone." And the light not only reveals Jesus—it is Jesus. Spurgeon continues, "You have not seen Christ, so as to be saved by his death, unless the light of the Spirit has revealed him to you as the great substitute for sinners." Further, "the way in which we receive light is by the Word of God," and "Christ himself is the essential Word."

This act of divine grace is the start of our walk with Jesus, just as day one is the first creation day. "It is a very early work of divine grace, I say, to show you that you are a sinner, and to reveal to you that you have a Savior; it is the first day's work, and I have no right to believe myself to be a new creation in God at all unless I have received light enough to know those two great and weighty facts—myself lost in Adam but saved in the second Adam, undone by sin but restored by the Savior's righteousness."

And this "day-one work" in the believer's heart is instantaneous, like the creation of light in verse 3: "Here let us observe that the work of giving spiritual light is instantaneous. No matter through what process you may go which you may conclude afterwards to have been preparatory to the light, and there is such a process, the Spirit of God brooded over the face of the waters before the light came in, yet the absolute flash which brings salvation is instantaneous. A man saved in a moment."

We see, then, the very gospel prefigured in the first three verses of the Bible.

Notes

130 Charles Haddon Spurgeon, "The First Day of Creation," The Spurgeon Center for Biblical Preaching at Midwestern Seminary, accessed September 13, 2019, https://www.spurgeon.org/resource-library/sermons/the-first-day-of-creation#flipbook.

131 Charles Haddon Spurgeon, "Light, Natural and Spiritual," The Spurgeon Center for Biblical Preaching at Midwestern Seminary, accessed September 13, 2019, https://www.spurgeon.org/resource-library/sermons/light-natural-and-spiritual#flipbook.

CHAPTER 15

Completion of Day One

Day one continues and finishes in verses 4 and 5:

> *⁴And God saw that the light was good. And God separated the light from the darkness. ⁵God called the light Day, and the darkness he called Night. And there was evening and there was morning, the first day.*

"God saw that the light was good." God indicates that His creation is good seven times. What does it mean that creation was "good"? Scripture does not elaborate. The Hebrew word translated "good" is *towb*, which is rendered in many different ways throughout the Bible. Many scholars, commentators, and readers take "good" to mean perfect. And by perfect they mean, for example, that there was no death in the world before the Fall, even plant or animal death, and there was no pain or difficulty of any kind. The main argument, I think, behind this interpretation is church tradition, but the reader by now knows how much weight I place on that. And I think the idea of no plant or animal death stretches credulity. What did the herbivores eat? Did the herbivorous animals and insects pick off just a few leaves of every plant they ate, allowing the plant to remain alive? And what did the carnivores eat? Were lions, with their teeth geared for tearing meat, content to eat plants before the Fall? Besides, if "good" means perfect, what does "very good" (verse 31) mean? You can't get more perfect than perfect. And in what sense are the stars, created on day four, "perfect"? And are volcanoes "perfect"? To me the reading of "good" as "perfect" seems like reading too much into the text. As John Walton puts it, "The conclusion is that anything that is negative in our experience did not exist in the primeval world. As popular as this view is, in reality the word never carries this sense of unadulterated, pristine perfection."[132] One other thing we can say, at least, is that God did not create evil. There is evil in the world, and God allows it to exist, but God did not create it. That, as Tremper Longman emphasizes, is another key difference with rival accounts. God's seven assessments of His creation as good demonstrates that evil did not originate with God and His creation.[133] In my opinion, the best interpretation of "good" is that creation worked the way God intended it to work.[134] Everything came out exactly as planned and envisioned. Put another way, as John Collins says, "Goodness means that it pleases him."[135]

Next, we see God separating the light from the darkness. Separation is a common manner of creation in the ancient Near Eastern accounts. Indeed, according to Gordon Wenham, "Creation as an act of separation between light and darkness, land and sea, and by the word of God all find parallels in Near Eastern theology."[136] Kenneth Mathews notes that with regard to Egypt, "Creation is a process of the unfolding of undifferentiated matter, the primeval Monad; thus Egyptian creation is more developmental than casual. Atum of Heliopolis, the creator-god, is the single source from which all emanates. The primeval hillock spontaneously emerges from the waters (Nun), and it is there that the creator-god is self-realized."[137] On a related point, in the ancient Near East, gods ruled the day and the night. Here, day and night are creations of God. God also names them, and in the ancient Near East naming was an act that signified ownership.[138] Finally, we have the refrain of "And there was evening and there was morning, the [nth] day." This refrain is repeated at the end of each of days one through six, establishing the literary device of the six-day creation week.

Notes

132 John H. Walton, *The Lost World of Adam and Eve* (Downers Grove, IL: IVP Academic, 2015), 53.

133 Tremper Longman III, *Genesis*, The Story of God Bible Commentary, eds. Tremper Longman III and Scot McKnight (Grand Rapids, MI: Zondervan, 2016), 35.

134 B. L. Gordon, "Scandal of the Evangelical Mind: A Biblical and Scientific Critique of Young-Earth Creationism," *Science, Religion and Culture* 1, no. 3 (2014): 144–73.

135 C. John Collins, *Genesis 1–4* (Phillipsburg, NJ: P&R, 2006), 75.

136 Gordon J. Wenham, *Genesis 1–15*, World Biblical Commentary (Grand Rapids, MI: Zondervan, 1987), xlviii.

137 Kenneth A. Mathews, *Genesis 1–11:26*, The New American Commentary (Nashville: B&H, 1996), 90.

138 A similar point is made in *Nelson's NKJV Study Bible* (Nashville: Thomas Nelson, 1997), 4.

CHAPTER 16

....

Days Two through Five

Day Two

⁶And God said, "Let there be an expanse in the midst of the waters, and let it separate the waters from the waters." ⁷And God made the expanse and separated the waters that were under the expanse from the waters that were above the expanse. And it was so. ⁸And God called the expanse Heaven. And there was evening and there was morning, the second day.

We've discussed the expanse before, so in this space I'll be brief. To the original audience, the expanse—an alternate translation of "canopy" is given in the ESV margin—was likely considered a solid dome that held back the sea above the dome, the cosmic sea. God again creates via separation, forming the cosmic sea from the earthly primeval sea. God then asserts ownership of heaven by naming it. And finally we get the standard refrain.

So here the Bible once again describes God emptying nature of all false gods. The sky was ruled by gods according to ancient Near Eastern thought. As Iain Provan explains, in ancient Egypt "the sky is represented by a goddess, Nut, who plays out her role in the cosmos by means of the sky"; and with regards to the peoples in the Syria-Palestine area, "the actions of the god Hadad (known as 'Ba'al' in the Old Testament and as Adad and Haddu elsewhere) were considered to have important consequences for life on earth. Hadad was the son of the high god El and the consort of the goddess Anat—a storm god who was the source of the rains that brought fertility to the land and enabled the agriculture cycle to continue."[139] In Genesis, the sky is a creation of God, who rules over it.

Day Three

⁹And God said, "Let the waters under the heavens be gathered together into one place, and let the dry land appear." And it was so. ¹⁰God called the dry land Earth, and the waters that were gathered together he called Seas. And God saw that it was good.

¹¹And God said, "Let the earth sprout vegetation, plants yielding seed, and fruit trees bearing fruit in which is their seed, each according to its kind, on the earth." And it was so. ¹²The earth brought forth vegetation, plants yielding seed according to their own kinds, and trees bearing fruit in which is their seed, each according to its kind. And God saw that it was good. ¹³And there was evening and there was morning, the third day.

We get a double dose of creation on day three, as land and plants appear. With respect to land, we see God taming the sea—a symbol of chaos and a pagan deity in the ancient Near East—and putting it in its place. This allows for the creation of a space for humans to live. Plants are split into three categories: vegetation, plants yielding seeds, and fruit-bearing trees. When God refers to the three types of plants, He is saying that He created all the various types of plants, and that they operate the way He designed them to. These various forms of plants are glorious in their own right. They also will provide sustenance for humans, and as such the creation of plants anticipates the creation of humans.

It is interesting that God creates plants (and later, land animals) via indirect means, having them spring forth from the earth. We should not be tempted to see any meaning here related to evolution. Rather, this is just another point of contact with the ancient Near Eastern myths, wherein creation sprang forth from the ground.[140] For example, in the *Eridu Genesis*, speaking of the creation of animals, it is written, "When An, Enlil, Enki, and Ninhursaga fashioned the dark-headed (people), they made the small animals (that came up) from (out of) the earth come from the earth in abundance."[141]

Much has been made of the word "kinds." Some think that this refers to a grouping above species, perhaps at the classification of family.[142] I think this is unsupported by the text. I don't think God is inserting modern scientific classification schemes into the text. Rather, I think the language here is merely phenomenological. The text is written to convey the natural sense in which the audience would have understood things to work. "Barley seeds give rise to barley plants. Pomegranate seeds give rise to pomegranate trees."[143] Barley seeds do not give rise to pomegranate trees.

Day Four

[14]And God said, "Let there be lights in the expanse of the heavens to separate the day from the night. And let them be for signs and for seasons, and for days and years, [15]and let them be lights in the expanse of the heavens to give light upon the earth." And it was so. [16]And God made the two great lights—the greater light to rule the day and the lesser light to rule the night—and

the stars. ¹⁷And God set them in the expanse of the heavens to give light on the earth, ¹⁸to rule over the day and over the night, and to separate the light from the darkness. And God saw that is was good. ¹⁹And there was evening and there was morning, the fourth day.

In keeping with the literary device of parallelism, on day four God fills the realm that was created on day one. And as is fitting, given their importance in the ancient world, the sun and moon and stars get a day all to themselves. Day four is also a prime example of the polemical aspects of Genesis 1, in particular Genesis' emphasis of monotheism over against the polytheism of the surrounding cultures. In the ancient Near East, the heavenly bodies were generally considered to be very important and powerful gods. As Bruce Waltke explains, "Whereas in the ancient Near Eastern myths, the sun and moon are principal deities, here they are nameless objects designed by the one Creator God to serve humanity."[144] And as Kenneth Mathews relates,

The moon deities of Mesopotamia are known from as early as the third millennium B.C., and they played an important role in cultic festivals into the first millennium B.C. Also West Semites paid homage to the moon; at Ugarit (1400–1200 B.C.) the moon deity was Yarik. The sun deity was of great importance to the Babylonians, who worshiped Shamash, and to the Egyptians, who paid homage to Re and Aton.[145]

Genesis, however, relegates these "deities" to mere creations of the one and only God. Many scholars have pointed out that Genesis 1:16 refuses to give the sun and the moon their proper names, which denoted them as gods by the surrounding cultures. Instead, the text refers to them simply as the greater and lesser lights. Furthermore, the stars were mentioned as a seeming afterthought. This was likely intentional, to strip them of their deity. There is no reason to worship these created things, the Bible is saying. Those deities that your neighbors worship? They are false. They are nothing. God created those things—they are material, not spiritual. They are created objects, not gods, and they were made to benefit you. There is no point in worshipping them. The sun, moon, and stars? Ha! God made them, and—dismissively, according to the nuance of the text—placed them. He doesn't even use their proper names.

Day Five

> [20]*And God said, "Let the waters swarm with swarms of living creatures, and let birds fly above the earth across the expanse of the heavens." [21]So God created the great sea creatures and every living creature that moves, with which the waters swarm, according to their kinds, and every winged bird according to its kind. And God saw that it was good. [22]And God blessed them, saying, "Be fruitful and multiply and fill the waters in the seas, and let birds multiply on the earth." [23]And there was evening and there was morning, the fifth day.*

Here we get the first creations of animals. In the ancient Near East creatures were routinely worshipped as gods, hence Moses's many exhortations against making idols of animals and worshipping them. And yet the Israelites, nevertheless, routinely did so. And thus, in addition to stating that God created all the fish in the sea and all the birds in the air, the author is saying that they are not to be worshipped. As Iain Provan puts it,

> *Creation is not to be worshipped, for it is not divine. There is separation between God and the world, and God, not the world, is to be worshipped. In general, for the peoples of the ancient Near East, "nature" was entirely personal—the very place where the gods were to be found. That which they perceived to*

be beyond the world was resolutely impersonal and ultimately irrelevant to their lives. Biblical faith, conversely, sees nature as impersonal, divesting it of the many gods who might be worshipped there. What lies beyond the world, however, is profoundly personal and profoundly relevant to life.[146]

One particular example is worth pointing out. Among the sea animals, the text specifically calls out "great sea creatures," which is translated "great sea-monsters" in some older translations such as the ASV. Many commentators explain that in the ancient Near East, the sea monsters are rival gods to be feared and defeated. In Genesis, by contrast, they are merely part of God's ordered creation. God is pointing out His dominion over the gods of the surrounding cultures, stripping them of their godhood by taking credit for their existence. God created them, then blessed them!

This blessing is another important aspect of day five. This is the first of many blessings God bestows in the Bible. There are many things we can take away from this blessing, and I'll mention just a couple of them here: God is good. He wills good for His creation, which was created out of love. Also, fruitfulness is a good thing. God wants His creation to spread and flourish. Why did God choose to make His first blessing on day five? For one thing, to show us that God cares for His animals, and we should too.

Notes

139 Iain Provan, *Seriously Dangerous Religion* (Waco, TX: Baylor University Press, 2014), 50–51.

140 Paul Copan and Douglas Jacoby, *Origins* (Nashville: Morgan James, 2019), 52.

141 *The Context of Scripture* (COS), volume 1, 1.158, trans. Thorkild Jacobsen.

142 A. Rahel Davidson Schafer, "The 'Kinds' of Genesis 1: What Is the Meaning of Min?" *Journal of the Adventist Theological Society* 14, no. 1 (2003): 86–100.

143 Vern S. Poythress, *Interpreting Eden* (Wheaton, IL: Crossway, 2019), 153.

144 Bruce K. Waltke, *Genesis* (Grand Rapids, MI: Zondervan Academic, 2001), 62.

145 Kenneth A. Mathews, *Genesis 1–11:26*, The New American Commentary (Nashville: B&H, 1996), 154.

146 Provan, *Seriously Dangerous Religion*, 31.

CHAPTER 17

Day Six

²⁴And God said, "Let the earth bring forth living creatures according to their kinds—livestock and creeping things, and beasts of the earth according to their kinds." And it was so. ²⁵And God made the beasts of the earth according to their kinds and the livestock according to their kinds, and everything that creeps on the ground according to its kind. And God saw that it was good.

²⁶Then God said, "Let us make man in our image, after our likeness. And let them have dominion over the fish in the sea and over the birds of the heavens and over the livestock and over all the earth and over every creeping thing that creeps on the earth." ²⁷So God created man in his own image, in the image of God he created him; male and female he created them. ²⁸And God blessed them. And God said to them, "Be fruitful and multiply and fill the earth and subdue it, and have dominion over the fish of the sea and over the birds of the heavens and over every living thing that moves on the earth." ²⁹And God said, "Behold, I have given you every plant yielding seed that is on the face of all the earth, and every tree with seed in its fruit. You shall have them for food. ³⁰And to every beast of the earth and to every bird of the heavens and to everything that creeps on the earth, everything that has the breath of life, I have given every green plant for food." And it was so. ³¹And God saw everything that he had made, and behold, it was very good. And there was evening and there was morning, the sixth day.

Day six begins with the creation of land animals (and insects). The analysis here is similar to that of the creation of sea and air animals in day five, so I won't say much on land-animal creation. But I'll note that man does not get a day all to himself. Although man is clearly the pinnacle of creation, he shares a day with land animals. It seems to me that God is reminding us that we too are creatures, not gods.

"Let us make man in our image, after our likeness." What is up with "us"? Well, that is a mystery. One view is that God is talking to a divine council from whom He receives input on decisions or to whom He delegates some responsibility in ruling and running the universe. Or perhaps He merely allows them a ringside seat. In ancient Near Eastern literature, there are of course divine courts and pantheons, and it appears there are divine councils as well. As Dennis Linscomb explains, "Other ANE parallels to the Genesis creation story describe the divine council. ... The concept of the divine council, or assembly of the gods, was a common religious theme in the cultures of Egypt, Mesopotamia, Canaan, Phoenicia, and Israel."[147]

So the Hebrews could have understood the phrase "Let us make" to be speaking of a divine council. There are some possible hints of such a council sprinkled through the Bible. Genesis 3:22 ("the man has become like one of us in knowing good and evil") uses similar language to 1:26 and may refer to a council. And later, regarding the Tower of Babel, the Lord says, "Come, let us go down and there confuse their language" (Genesis 11:7). This implies He is working with, or at least in the company of, others. Job 1:6 and 2:1 talk of the "sons of God" (presumably angelic beings) who, along with Satan, present themselves before the Lord in an assembly. Jeremiah 23:18 says, "For who among them has stood in the council of the LORD to see and to hear his word, or who has paid attention to his word and listened?" It is well understood that, at the least, God is surrounded by lots of angels and heavenly beings; see for example 1 Kings 22:19, which says, "I saw the LORD sitting on his throne, and all the host of heaven standing beside him on his right hand and on his left." And Job 38:7 testifies that "all the sons of God shouted for joy" at the creation. It is possible that God chooses to rule with the assistance of, or at least in the presence of, a council.

Another view is that God is merely using a royal plural. Basically, He is reflecting majesty upon Himself by talking about Himself in a plural sense. This doesn't seem likely to me, as I haven't been able to find any other place in Scripture where God clearly does this.

A third possibility, and the one that I favor (although the first view seems quite plausible to me as well), is that God is talking about the Trinity. As we've established, all three members take part in creation. God the Father saying to Jesus and the Holy Spirit, "Let us make," seems like the simplest answer to me. One other reason to favor the Trinity view is the precise language in verse 26. It says, "make man in our image." It is generally agreed that we are made in God's image, not the image of angels, and this is made explicit in verse 27 ("in his own image"). "Us," then, appears to be referring to the Trinity.

Continuing on with verse 26, the text emphasizes that we are made in God's "image" and "likeness." What does this actually mean? Let's take "image" first. Once more, we come to an area of vigorous debate. The traditional view is that being made in the image of God means that we share certain attributes with God.[148] Proponents will point to the characteristics that set us apart from the rest of creation: our intelligence, reason, morality, and creativity. To me, this seriously misses the mark. For one thing, these attributes we cherish are mere faint shadows of what God possesses. Take intelligence, for example. Assume for ease of discussion that God's intelligence is bounded, and that we measure intelligence on a scale of 0 (no intelligence) to 1,000,000. If God's intelligence is a perfect 1,000,000, then ours couldn't be higher than a 4. Gosh, the other day I had trouble figuring out how to use a new can opener. Are we really like God with respect to intelligence? But it gets worse. A chimp's intelligence, in our example, would come in at 3. So a chimp is 3, a human is 4, and God is 1,000,000. Is that what God meant by making us in His image? Even with respect to morality, some higher animals have been known to act in ways that we would view as moral. Dogs show loyalty to their masters, elephants grieve over the bones of their family members, primates share food, mothers of all sorts care for their young. Also, we have many characteristics that we do not share with God. We counter God's image in many ways. Even before the Fall, we had a penchant for disobedience; had it been otherwise, Adam and Eve would not have disobeyed God. Yet God is perfectly obedient, as Jesus was perfectly obedient to the Father "to the point of death, even death on a cross" (Philippians 2:8). So this interpretation simply does not work, in my view.

There is another interpretation that is more faithful to both the original intent of the author and to biblical theology: We are made in the image of God in the sense that we represent God. We are, in effect, images of Him. This interpretation is grounded in the cultural environment of the ancient Near East, and I think it is clearly how the original audience would have understood the term. In the ancient Near East, "kings were divine image-bearers, appointed representatives of God on earth,"[149] and often placed statues of themselves throughout and at the edges of their territory. These images of the king served to show his dominion over the territory. Tellingly, "both terms, [image] and [likeness], are found together in a ninth century old Aramaic inscription from Tell Fakhariyeh [Northeast Syria] to describe the statue of King Haddu-yisi, the oldest pairing of these terms yet known in Aramaic."[150] So, then, this interpretation conveys that

humanity corporately functions as God's vice-regents—stewards
who are charged with subduing and ruling as articulated in the
very context in which the image is granted (Gen 1:26–30). As a
corporate designation, it differentiates humanity from all other
creatures and species. Those capacities that can be discussed
neurologically (self-awareness, God-awareness, etc.) may well be
understood to allow us to carry out this task, but they would not
themselves define the image of God.[151]

The answer to the question of what the image is, then, is given in the very same verse where "image" is introduced—it is the function of being God's delegated representatives on earth. And this role applies to all of us. In the ancient Near East, the image of a god was bestowed by that god onto a king. God bestows His image on each and every one of us. This is another striking contrast to the competing creation accounts. In Genesis, each human being is equally valued by God. We are all kings.

What are we to accomplish as His representatives? To be sure, taking proper care of His creation by being good stewards of His world. But while this world is an end in itself in terms of reflecting God's glory, it is also a means to an end. This world will end. God's ultimate goal is to gather saints who will worship Him and be in a loving relationship with Him for eternity. As it says in Revelation 21:3, "He will dwell with them, and they will be his people, and God himself will be with them as their God."

Being God's representative means working to fulfill God's purpose. So being God's representative means reflecting Jesus's love to the world, such that believers are heartened and encouraged, but also so that those who have not heard the gospel, or those who have heard it but have not accepted it, might be born again. According to New Testament theology, we are God's image now in the sense that God lives inside us, and consequently we are "the light of the world" (Matthew 5:14). And we are His representatives in that we follow

Jesus's command: "Go therefore and made disciples of all nations" (Matthew 28:19). As God's images, we reflect His glory and allow Him to work through us to achieve His divine plan.

What about the meaning of "likeness"? John Collins points out that in Hebrew, "likeness" is "a more general term for 'resemblance,' without saying what kind of resemblance is in view (that is inferred from the context)."[152] Bruce Waltke argues that the context here is to emphasize that we are like God, but we are not gods: "Whereas the image of the deity is equated with the deity itself in the ancient Near East, the word *likeness* serves to clearly distinguish God from humans in the biblical worldview."[153]

I briefly referenced subduing and ruling above. We were created to "have dominion" (verse 26) and to "subdue" (verse 28) the earth. What the phrase "and let them have dominion" highlights is that one purpose of creation is to work for us, for our benefit. We are on top of the earthly totem pole. This is manifestly not a license to plunder the earth, however. The earth and all that is in it belongs to God. As David Platt has remarked, "The one who created us, owns us."[154] This not only refers to humans, but to all of creation. God owns all of creation. We are merely stewards, and we are charged with managing well what has been entrusted to us. And indeed the original audience would have understood this, as the "vocation of kings in the context of the ancient world involved not only ruling and subduing but also looking after the welfare of their subjects and ensuring justice for all."[155]

Verse 27 is a poetic and elaborate replacement for "and it was so": "So God created man in his own image, in the image of God he created him; male and female he created them." This emphasizes that man is the pinnacle of creation, the crowning achievement. This is the climax of the chapter. It also speaks to the equality of women and men. Both are made in God's image—"man" in 1:26a is in a grammatical form such that it refers to humanity in general, and then male and female are called out specifically to make sure we don't miss the point.

Right after the climax is the blessing of humans and the provision of food for man and for animal. An important message in the text here is that God provides for us. This is in stark contrast to the creation narratives of the ancient Near East, where humans were created in order to do the work of the gods. Rather than humans providing for the gods, God provides for humans. As Paul notes in Acts 17:25, God is not "served by human hands, as though he needed anything, since he himself gives to all mankind life and breath and everything." Why does God provide for us? Because He loves us. And implied in provision and love is relationship. What we see in the account of the creation of man, then, is a God who cares for us and loves us, and who wants us to reflect His love to others so that more of us may be with Him in eternity, where we "will worship the Father in spirit and truth" (John 4:23). In a real sense, then, Genesis 1 begins to set the table for John 3:16—"For God so loved the world, that he gave his only Son, that whoever believes in him should not perish but have eternal life."

Notes

147 Dennis Linscomb, "The Ancient Near Eastern Context of the Genesis Creation and Flood Stories and Its Impact on Biblical Inspiration," Academia, January 4, 2016, https://www.academia.edu/20019677/The_Ancient_Near_Eastern_Context_of_the_Genesis_Creation_and_Flood_Stories_and_Its_Impact_on_Biblical_Inspiration.

148 For a thorough discussion of the state of scholarship on this issue as of the late 1960s, see D. J. A. Clines, "The Image of God in Man," *Tyndale Bulletin* 19 (1968): 53–103.

149 Peter Enns, *The Evolution of Adam* (Grand Rapids, MI: Brazos, 2012), xv.

150 Gordon Wenham, *Genesis 1–15*, World Biblical Commentary (Grand Rapids, MI: Zondervan, 1987), 29.

151 John Walton, *The Lost World of Adam and Eve* (Downers Grove, IL: IVP Academic, 2015), 194.

152 C. John Collins, *Genesis 1–4* (Phillipsburg, NJ: P&R, 2006), 65.

153 Bruce K. Waltke, *Genesis* (Grand Rapids, MI: Zondervan Academic, 2001), 66.

154 David Platt, "In the Beginning, God (Genesis 1:1)," Podcast #246, *Pray the Word*, April 13, 2018, https://radical.net/podcast/246-in-the-beginning-god-genesis-11.

155 Iain Provan, *Seriously Dangerous Religion* (Waco, TX: Baylor University Press, 2014), 225.

CHAPTER 18

···

Day Seven

2:1 Thus the heavens and the earth were finished, and all the host of them. 2And on the seventh day God finished his work that he had done, and he rested on the seventh day from all his work that he had done. 3So God blessed the seventh day and made it holy, because on it God rested from all his work that he had done in creation.

Creation is finished, and God rests. As many scholars have pointed out, the Hebrew translated here as "rest" does not mean vacation. It most nearly means to cease working. And the author of Genesis is quick to emphasize that it is the work of creation, not any of God's other work, that He ceases. The implication is that there is a lot of other work that God continues to do; God is an active, personal God, engaged in the world and in our lives. He does not rest from His work of salvation nor in directing events to bring about His purposes. To rest, for God, involves sitting on His throne and getting down to business. As Jesus said in the Gospel of John, "My Father is working until now, and I am working" (John 5:17). Indeed, the main purpose of creation is to provide Him with a world to rule and with humans to be in relationship with, culminating with a multitude of saints who shall praise and worship Him in eternity. In a real sense, then, the purpose of creation is rest, and "God has ordered the cosmos with the purpose of taking up his residence in it and ruling over it. Day seven is the reason for days one through six. It is the fulfillment of God's purpose."[156] While the creation of man is the climax of the creation story, God's rest is the resolution. This is similar to how Jesus's resurrection is the climax of the entire Bible, but the establishment of the new Jerusalem in the last two chapters of Revelation is the resolution. In a way, the creation of man prefigured man being born again in Jesus, and God's rest on day seven prefigures His kingdom in eternity.

We can see this now with the benefit of the New Testament. What would the original audience have understood? Here is where the figure of the world as a temple comes into focus. As Iain Provan explains,

> *It is critical here to remember the close connection between temple and cosmos in the ancient mind and the marked similarity between ancient Near Eastern texts concerning the making of the world and those concerning the construction of temples. In both kinds of text, a story is told of the emergence of a stable and ordered environment in which divinity could find "rest," enjoying (along with his worshippers) the peace and security of the cosmos. The temple-dedication ceremonies that ended in this divine rest often lasted seven days.*[157]

God's presence on earth is a key theme in the Bible. In Genesis, the earth is God's temple, which implies that He is omnipresent. Later in the Old Testament, God dwells more explicitly in the tabernacle and then in the Jerusalem temple. In the New Testament, God dwells in Jesus, who is God, and then in the hearts of Christians. Finally, He will dwell in the new Jerusalem.

At the conclusion of the creation process, God blessed the seventh day and made it holy. He set the day apart. This gives justification for the implementation of a weekly Sabbath (see Exodus 20:11). The act of blessing a day seems a bit hard to understand. I liken it to blessing a marriage. The blessing is actually for the husband and wife, for their relationship with each other. In the same way, I think when God blesses the Sabbath day He is implicitly blessing us in our efforts to use that day to commune with Him. In this way, God invites us into relationship with Him and into His Sabbath rest. As the author of Hebrews states, "So then, there remains a Sabbath rest for the people of God, for whoever has entered God's rest has also rested from his works as God did from his" (Hebrews 4:9–10). I believe this refers to rest not only in heaven but also here on earth in "the peace of God, which surpasses all understanding" (Philippians 4:7) and guards our hearts and minds in Christ Jesus.

Notes

156   John Walton, *The Lost World of Adam and Eve* (Downers Grove, IL: IVP Academic, 2015), 49.

157   Iain Provan, *Seriously Dangerous Religion* (Waco, TX: Baylor University Press, 2014), 59.

CHAPTER 19

Genealogies, Redux

Now that we have a figurative interpretation, let's begin to tie up a couple of loose ends before closing the book on creation.

Earlier, when I looked at Genesis 1 from a literal viewpoint, I examined the genealogies of the Bible. I determined that a literal analysis of the genealogies showed that they could not be used to precisely date the earth, and while in theory they could allow for very old origins for humanity, they did seem to suggest that humanity's origins were a fair bit more recent than science reveals. When I looked at the genealogies through a figurative window, my remaining uneasiness went away. Using a figurative lens to assess the genealogies eliminates any contradiction between them and modern science. Figurative considerations seem to be the best explanation for the incompleteness of the genealogies, particularly the ones in Genesis. Accuracy was not the goal.

In the ancient world, the purpose of genealogies was not to be strictly literal. They were not "constructed for purely genetic-historical purposes."[158] I am not saying that the people in the biblical genealogies weren't real. To be clear, I believe the people mentioned in the genealogies were real people. I believe it is also true that the genealogies had other purposes and were shaped and molded to suit those purposes. As Bruce Gordon concludes, "The purpose of the

Genesis genealogies is not to allow a calculation of elapsed time—this is an abuse of them—rather, it is to establish lines of descent and also to emphasize the fact, drummed home by the recurrent phrase 'and he died,' that death was a consequence of the sin of Adam and Eve."[159] And as George Isham writes, "In ancient times, genealogies were used to preserve all sorts of information, not just biological descent. Thus, we might expect biblical genealogies to contain data about the social, geographic, and political status of Israel's ancestors."[160] Perhaps the most important purpose of the biblical genealogies was establishing the humanity of Jesus and validating His lineage back through David and Abraham, but there were likely other purposes as well. As such, the genealogies were shaped and molded for other ends than reporting pure history.

There are many clues that there are figurative elements to the genealogies. One obvious clue is the long lifespans. Large numbers here could be used to denote the importance of these individuals. The long ages could also have served a political purpose. The Hebrews lived in the shadow of larger cultures. One of those was the Sumerians. The Sumerians had a king list, now commonly referred to as the *Sumerian King List*, which we referenced earlier and which is older than Genesis. It gives the names of Sumer's former kings and the length of their reigns. The list starts with eight, nine, or ten kings, depending upon the version. These kings had exceedingly long lifespans—one is said to have reigned for over 43,000 years! But then comes a great flood. After the flood the list of kings continues, but the lifespans get much shorter. This pattern matches Genesis quite well. The genealogies in Genesis 5 and 11 may have been patterned after the *Sumerian King List*. They also may have been patterned after the *Eridu Genesis*, which offers a list of kings who also enjoyed exceptionally long reigns and 100-year childhoods.[161] Compare this with the early Genesis patriarchs who didn't have children until they were older than 100. Perhaps this was the Hebrews asserting and emphasizing that they, too, had a deep cultural heritage, using a context that the original hearers and readers would have understood and identified with. As K. A. Kitchen explains, "Gen. 1–11 is the Hebrew answer on how to present 'prehistory/protohistory.' ... The Hebrew genealogies became telescoped through time, keeping a representative number, with possible man/clan figures spread along the now invisible intervals of the longer lines."[162]

One interesting thing to note here is that the eight pre-flood members of the *Sumerian King List* each had ages with five digits. Each of the ten patriarchs in the Genesis 5 genealogy had ages with three digits. Three and five are symbolic numbers in the ancient world and in the Bible.

Indeed, there is likely a great deal of symbolism in the genealogies in the Bible, although the exact nature of the symbolism is mysterious. The ages of the ten patriarchs is a prime example. For each, there are three numbers presented—the age at which they begat a descendant, the number of years they lived after that, and their age at death (or, in the case of Enoch, the age he "walked with God" [Genesis 5:22]). This provides 30 numbers. As Jim Stump explains, all 30 of those numbers end in 0, 2, 5, 7, or 9.[163] So out of ten possible digits, all the numbers end in one of a subset of five digits. The chance of this happening naturally is very small. So there is obviously something going on here besides a straight reporting of history. Unfortunately, no one to my knowledge has "cracked the code" and figured out the meaning of the numbers.

Also note that there are ten members in each of the genealogies of Genesis 5 (Adam to Noah) and Genesis 11 (Noah to Abram). This seems like quite a coincidence and again implies that the genealogies were edited to serve a purpose. In the Genesis 5 genealogy, the seventh member—there is that number seven again—is distinctive. This is Enoch, who is called out for his holiness. He did not die but rather "walked with God, and he was not, for God took him" (Genesis 5:24). Enoch is from the godly line of Adam, the line of Adam's son Seth, of whom it is written in Genesis 4, "At that time people began to call upon the name of the LORD" (Genesis 4:26). It is interesting that the seventh member of Adam's line through Cain, the ungodly line, is called out as well, but for the opposite reason. Lamech brags to his two wives about his unbridled vengeance and violence—"I have killed a man for wounding me, a young man for striking me" (Genesis 4:23). The contrast between this violent murderer and a man who was spirited straight to heaven is striking. The third members—and three is another symbolic number in the Bible—of the respective genealogies are also called out for special attention. In the godly line through Seth, the third member is Seth's son Enosh, who was born at the "time people began to call upon the name of the LORD" (Genesis 4:26). The third member of the line through Cain is Cain's son Enoch (not to be confused with the Enoch that walked with God). Cain named a city after Enoch. God had made Cain a "wanderer on the earth" (Genesis 4:12), so the building of this city appears to have been an act of defiance against God. So again, the author may have been using the genealogies to show the divergence between the kingdom of God on earth and the surrounding world of ungodly men.

Symmetry and symbolic numbers seem to have been important in the New Testament as well. Matthew's genealogies were shaped such that each of the three sections—Abraham to David, David to the Babylonian captivity, and the Babylonian captivity to Jesus— have 14 members. And 14 itself is a multiple of the symbolic number seven. In the genealogy of Luke 3, there are 78 members, "implying a symbolically perfect seventy-seven generations."[164] So the symbolic numbers three and seven are again prominent. Whatever the precise intention of the symmetry and symbolism, it seems that the authors were fine with sacrificing historical precision in order to further other aims.

One other point about genealogies in Genesis is that they play an important role in the structure of the narrative. They form the backbone of Genesis. Given this role, the genealogies would be needed for other purposes besides just reporting literal history.

Considering all of the above, I became quite satisfied that the genealogies of the Bible do not assert any particular age for the earth.

Notes

158 Tremper Longman III and John H. Walton, *The Lost World of the Flood* (Downers Grove, IL: IVP Academic, 2018), 107.

159 B. L. Gordon, "Scandal of the Evangelical Mind: A Biblical and Scientific Critique of Young-Earth Creationism," *Science, Religion and Culture* 1, no. 3 (2014): 144–73.

160 George F. Isham, *Bible Chronology and the Sumerian King List* (self-pub., 2014), 23.

161 Thorkild Jacobsen, "The Eridu Genesis," *Journal of Biblical Literature* 100, no. 4 (1981): 513–29.

162 K. A. Kitchen, *On the Reliability of the Old Testament* (Grand Rapids, MI: Eerdmans, 2003), 447.

163 Jim Stump, "Long Life Spans in Genesis: Literal or Symbolic?" Biologos, October 5, 2017, https://biologos.org/articles/long-life-spans-in-genesis-literal-or-symbolic.

164 Daniel C. Harlow, "After Adam: Reading Genesis in an Age of Evolutionary Science," *Journal of the American Scientific Affiliation* 62, no. 3 (2010): 179–95.

CHAPTER 20

··

Consistency with
Other Bible Passages

Lastly, we need to make sure that the interpretation of Genesis 1 that I've given does not conflict with other passages in the Bible. The two passages that I think we need to consider most closely are Exodus 20:8–11 and Exodus 31:12–17, which command the Israelites to keep the Sabbath.

Exodus 20:11

20:8Remember the Sabbath day, to keep it holy. 9Six days you shall labor, and do all your work, 10but the seventh day is a Sabbath to the LORD your God. On it you shall not do any work, you, or your son, or your daughter, your male servant, or your female servant, or your livestock, or the sojourner who is within your gates. 11For in six days the LORD made heaven and earth, the sea, and all that is in them, and rested on the seventh day. Therefore the LORD blessed the Sabbath day and made it holy.

The context here is that God is giving the Ten Commandments to Israel. In this fourth commandment, God is instituting the Sabbath for His people. On the surface, verse 11 poses a challenge. It seems to literally state that the earth was created in six days. However, when we brush off the surface dust and take a look at the passage in the light of a figurative interpretation of Genesis 1, we see that verse 11 is consistent with such an interpretation and is not in contradiction with science.

It is important to understand that Exodus 20:11 is not interpreting Genesis 1. Rather, in a roundabout way, Genesis 1 interprets and explains the Sabbath. The author is using Genesis 1 as support and explanation for the implementation of the Sabbath. Indeed, as we saw in an earlier chapter, the creation days were set up as a figurative device, in part to provide force and clarity to a key message of the text, the importance and sanctity of the Sabbath. One of the purposes of the "days" motif was to set up the anthropomorphism of God going about a human workweek. This language, in turn, would strongly support the institution of the Sabbath. The text here in Exodus refers back to the creation days of Genesis 1 in order to explain the fourth commandment in familiar terms. God worked for six days and rested for one, so you can and should work for six days and rest for one.

Exodus 20:11 says that Genesis 1 undergirds the Sabbath. As Copan and Jacoby put it, "(Genesis) 1 provides a theology of the Sabbath."[165] In this light, we see that the first part of verse 11 is not giving an interpretation of Genesis 1 but referring back to Genesis 1. It is not teaching about Genesis 1—it is invoking Genesis 1: "For in six days the LORD made heaven and earth, the sea, and all that is in them, and rested on the seventh day." This verse refers to Genesis 1 in its entirety. It is describing the way creation was portrayed in Genesis 1. It refers to the truth of Genesis 1, truth that was expressed figuratively.

In a real sense, then, Exodus 20:11 is a placeholder for everything Genesis 1 taught. It is saying, "Hey, based on what you were taught in Genesis 1, you must keep the Sabbath holy." We can thus replace 20:11 with "the meaning of Genesis 1." But Genesis 1 has a figurative meaning, not a literal meaning. As we saw earlier, we can summarize what was taught in Genesis 1 by saying that the Lord alone is God. He created the universe and everything in it to display His glory and to provide Himself with a world to rule and with humans to be in relationship with; this will culminate with a multitude of saints praising and worshipping Him in eternity. He now sits on His throne, engaged in His work of salvation. So this is what it means to say, "For in six days the LORD made heaven and earth, the sea, and all that is in them, and rested on the seventh day."

Let's now read Exodus 20:8–11 anew, substituting in the meaning of Genesis 1:

> *Remember the Sabbath day, to keep it holy. Six days you shall labor, and do all your work, but the seventh day is a Sabbath to the Lord your God. On it you shall not do any work, you, or your son, or your daughter, your male servant, or your female servant, or your livestock, or the sojourner who is within your gates. For the Lord, the one and only God, the King of the universe, made the heavens and the earth for His glory, to provide Him with a world to rule and with humans to be in relationship with, to culminate with a multitude of saints praising and worshipping Him in eternity. He now sits on His throne and engages in His salvific work. Therefore the Lord blessed the Sabbath day, the culmination and resolution of creation. The Sabbath day, which is continuing even now, is holy.*

Now we can access the meaning of the passage. The Lord blesses the Sabbath day and makes it holy because it is part of how God executes His plan, working with and through His people. The text is saying, in effect: "Listen, people. Remember the truth you learned in Genesis 1. This is how we apply it. This is how we live it."

Let's go back to the top of the passage. The Israelites had to participate in the Sabbath and keep it holy. To do this, they had to keep themselves holy—to set themselves apart for God. They had to acknowledge that they belonged to Him. The focus of their lives was to worship Him, as they were created to do. To be in relationship with Him, as they were created to be. To depend upon Him for their needs, as they were created to do. To reflect His glory to the world as His representatives, as they were created to do. To participate in His work of salvation, as they were created to do. Just as the purpose of the six creation days was the seventh day, the purpose of the Israelites' lives was their relationship with their Lord.

A function of the Sabbath was to remind the Israelites of the preceding paragraph. Even more, the Sabbath was a vehicle for the Israelites to put the preceding paragraph into action. The Sabbath was a day for the Israelites to spend extra time in worship of God. The Sabbath was a day for them to commune with God, deepening their relationship with Him. The Sabbath was a day when they were explicitly to put down their work, relying on God—above, beyond, and instead of their own labors—to provide for their needs. The observance of the Sabbath would be a sign for the world, such that the world could recognize that God was present in the midst of the Israelites, and thereby, the Israelites were to participate in God's work of salvation for the world.

A key point for us to remember is that the seventh day has not ended yet. God's rule and His work of salvation continue on. And while we are no longer required to keep the strictures of the Sabbath (see Colossians 2:16, "Let no one pass judgment on you ... with regard to ... a Sabbath"), the spirit of the commandment still holds true and is still relevant to us today. God calls us, as members of His kingdom, to set ourselves apart for Him and to participate in His ongoing work of rule and salvation by worshipping Him, loving Him, relying on Him, and projecting His glory to the world as His representatives.

In conclusion, verse 11 does not mean that the six creation days are to be taken literally. The passage is instituting the Sabbath observance, and in so doing refers back to and cites Genesis 1 for support and explanation. Exodus 20:11 simply says, "This is what is written in Genesis 1." Exodus 20:11 is not offering an interpretation of Genesis 1 as being literal or figurative. Exodus is affirming the truth of Genesis 1, truth that was expressed figuratively. Just because an author affirms the truth of a verse does not mean that that verse has to be interpreted literally. Figuratively expressed truth is truth too, just as much as literally expressed truth. As Douglas Stuart, in his extensive commentary on Exodus, notes, "The wording of the commandment, however, does not necessarily endorse a literal six-day creation any more than the wording of Gen 1 itself does."[166]

Exodus 31:17

Later on in Exodus, the Lord instructs Moses to reemphasize the Sabbath with the Israelites:

31:12And the LORD said to Moses, 13"You are to speak to the people of Israel and say, 'Above all you shall keep my Sabbaths, for this is a sign between me and you throughout your generations, that you may know that I, the LORD, sanctify you. 14You shall keep the Sabbath, because it is holy for you. Everyone who profanes it shall be put to death. Whoever does any work on it, that soul shall be cut off from among his people. 15Six days shall work be done, but the seventh day is a Sabbath of solemn rest, holy to the LORD. Whoever does any work on the Sabbath day shall be put to death. 16Therefore the people of Israel shall keep the Sabbath, observing the Sabbath throughout their generations, as a covenant forever. 17It is a sign forever between me and the people of Israel that in six days the LORD made heaven and earth, and on the seventh day he rested and was refreshed.'"

In verse 13 we see that the Sabbath is a sign between God and the Israelites, a way for them to remember that, as Genesis 1 teaches, God made them and set them apart for relationship with Him and to be His representatives. In verse 14 the Israelites are told they are not just to acknowledge such, but to participate in the relationship via Sabbath observance. They are to keep the Sabbath because it is holy for them. The Sabbath is holy for them because it is holy for God and because they are in relationship with a holy God.

In both verses 14 and 15, God institutes the death penalty for profaning the Sabbath. This seems extreme, but merely highlights that profaning the Sabbath is an extreme thing to do. I imagine that a Levitical priest may have explained it to a struggling Israelite thusly:

A holy God created you to be in relationship with Him, and you are part of the people group that He specifically designated to be His light to the nations. The Creator of the universe cares for you and provides for you. He has instituted the Sabbath as a key means for you to commune with Him. The Sabbath was made for you.[167] By disregarding the Sabbath, you are walking away from Him, rejecting Him—rejecting a loving God who has made Himself known to you and has chosen you to be one of His people! This is supremely disrespectful and is akin to apostasy. By rejecting the Sabbath, you are rejecting your God and your people and can no longer be counted as one of us.

And this is not just an Old Testament thing. In the New Testament, rejecting God leads to eternal death: "But whoever does not believe is condemned already, because he has not believed in the name of the only Son of God" (John 3:18).

Next we see in verse 16 that, indeed, the Sabbath is a covenant. Keeping the Sabbath meant staying in the covenant relationship with God. Breaking the Sabbath meant exiting the relationship, no longer being party to the covenant. Similarly, as Brevard Childs explains, the Sabbath "is a reminder both to God and Israel of the eternal covenantal relationship which was the ultimate purpose of creation."[168]

And now we arrive at verse 17. As for God's side of the covenant, He fulfilled His part at creation when He finished His work and entered into His rest, and all that that entails, which continues to this day. This was portrayed in Genesis 1 in a figurative sense as a six-day workweek followed by a day of rest, and the Exodus passage refers to that story, and to the truth of that story, to show that God has kept the covenant.

More generally, the Sabbath was a sign for the Israelites. It pointed to the truth of Genesis 1—truth that was portrayed figuratively. God made us, and He made us that we might have a relationship with Him and serve as His representatives in the world. The Sabbath is a reminder that Genesis 1, as told figuratively, is truth. Creation in six days is the way that these truths were presented in Genesis 1, and so Exodus 31:17 just picks up on that story. As in Exodus 20:11, Exodus 31:17 is just citing Genesis 1. It is not interpreting Genesis 1 as being either literal or figurative.

Assorted New Testament Passages

There are a few New Testament passages that are held up by some as evidence of six-day creation, but I am not persuaded by any of the associated arguments.

One example is Mark 10:6 where Jesus, in explaining marriage and divorce, says that "from the beginning of creation, 'God made them male and female.'" The YEC argument seems to be that this shows that humans were made at the beginning of creation, and so creation was a compact event on the order of a week rather than billions of years. But I don't think that is the best way to read the text. First of all, if we are to take it very literally, Jesus is saying that He made man and woman on day one (the beginning) of creation. Which is not what Genesis 1 says. So even if we take the verse hyper-literally, as the YEC advocates demand, the verse does not support their claim. But more broadly speaking, in this passage (and in the parallel passage of Matthew 19:4) Jesus is not teaching about creation; He is teaching about marriage. So let's instead look at what Jesus is doing here. Jesus is pointing the audience to a time before the laws about divorce given by Moses. Yes, Jesus is saying, Moses allowed divorce, but that was not God's intention for marriage when He created the institution. Jesus is saying, "Don't look to Moses; look back further than Moses, back to early Genesis." Jesus is citing the truth of Genesis 1:27 and 5:2 to teach about marriage. I don't think He is telling us that Genesis 1:27 happened 6,000 years ago, and I don't think He is making a case as to the literal or figurative nature of the Genesis 1 creation account. Finally, note that although Jesus is referencing Genesis 1:27 and 5:2, in a sense He may be alluding back further, even before Genesis 1:1, to when God conceived the world and decided to create it.

Even if we accept the YEC interpretation—and I do not think that is warranted at all—there are further avenues to reject a contradiction in the text. One is that Jesus was using the science of the day, accommodating to His audience, who would undoubtedly have failed to comprehend the concept that the earth was billions of years old. Another possibility is that Jesus, being fully human (as well as fully God), did not know the age of the earth. I don't personally subscribe to this viewpoint, but I think it is a legitimate opinion. When Jesus was a small child, I presume He did not understand physics and similar fields of study. As He got older He "increased in wisdom" (Luke 2:52), but did He eventually obtain all the knowledge that He had a right to as God? I'm not certain. In Matthew 24:36, a teaching on the end times, Jesus says that "concerning that day and hour no one knows, not even the angels of heaven, nor the Son, but the Father only." So Jesus's knowledge in some matters was constricted. Perhaps perfect knowledge was one of the prerogatives that He gave up when

He "emptied himself, by taking the form of a servant, being born in the likeness of men" (Philippians 2:7). Perhaps He even gave up knowledge of His own prior actions as God. How then did He know about, say, the personal history of the woman at the well in John 4? Perhaps Jesus knew only what the Holy Spirit told Him. The incarnation is a mystery, and we shouldn't be too confident in our attempts to fully understand it.

Another favorite passage of YEC advocates is Luke 11:50; here Jesus, speaking about the Jewish leaders of the day, says that "the blood of all the prophets, shed from the foundation of the world, may be charged against this generation." Here, I don't believe that He is speaking technically and concretely and literally about the creation of man being close in time to the creation of the universe. I don't think He intends to teach us anything about the subject of the scientific timing of creation. Rather, I think He is artfully and poetically saying that the current generation would be judged for the murders of all the prophets that had ever lived. (That judgment may have been fulfilled through the fall of Jerusalem in AD 70.)[169]

Another example is Hebrews 4:3. The author there is teaching about the vital importance of faith as the means by which we enter God's rest, which was established at the end of the creation account of Genesis 1. In the midst of this discourse, he comments that "his works were finished from the foundation of the world." The context is that God, who had already entered His rest, swore that He would not allow the Israelites who rebelled in the desert to enter that rest with Him.

The YEC argument, I believe, is that the phrase "his works were finished from the foundation of the world" implies that day seven was close in time to days one through six. But the "foundation of the world" could be taken to mean the end of the creation account, rather than day one. In any event, I don't think the author is teaching about the genre of Genesis 1 or the literal versus figurative nature of it. I think that the author is merely making the point that God's rest began after His creative work, which was obviously earlier in time than when the Israelites were in the desert. In doing so, he refers back to Genesis 1. He does not interpret Genesis 1, but rather employs the truth contained in Genesis 1.

There are other passages that are argued by some to apply to six-day creation. As with those just discussed, I do not see any authoritatively teaching a literal interpretation of Genesis 1. In short, I see no conflicts between my reading of Genesis 1 and the rest of Scripture.

This study of passages from Exodus and the New Testament wrapped up my investigation of Genesis 1. At this point, I let go a sigh of relief. I had successfully tackled one issue. And as a bonus, the tools I acquired—the consideration of ancient Near East literature and of figurative interpretations—could be applied to other issues. But I knew I had harder challenges ahead. At this time I was about halfway through looking into the flood, and it was giving me problems. In multiple ways, the flood was proving to be more difficult to investigate than creation.

Notes

165   Paul Copan and Douglas Jacoby, *Origins* (Nashville: Morgan James, 2019), 76.

166   Douglas K. Stuart, *Exodus*, The New American Commentary (Nashville: B&H, 2006), 460.

167   As Jesus would later say in Mark 2:27.

168   Brevard S. Childs, *Exodus* (London: SCM, 1974), 416.

169   As to the sacking of Jerusalem being the punishment Christ was referring to, see John MacArthur, *The MacArthur Study Bible* (Wheaton, IL: Crossway, 2010), 1403.

PART III

The Flood

CHAPTER 21

Dinosaurs Again

"Daddy, did the dinosaurs go extinct in Noah's flood?"

I tried to put him off, explaining that I was busy getting ready to go to work and that he had to leave for school soon, but Sam (then 10 years old) was very persistent. He needed me to settle an argument he was having with his sister Clare (then 11 years old). Clare insisted that the dinosaurs went extinct due to a meteor. Sam, pure in heart, was adamant that they died in the flood, because that is what his teacher told him. I gently told Sam I thought dinosaurs lived a long time ago and were all gone by the time of the flood. With regard to his teacher (a kind and Spirit-filled woman whom Sam loved), I explained that his teacher and I simply had different opinions.

We sure did have different opinions. And I was struggling with how my conviction that there was no global flood meshed with what the Bible was telling me. More to the point, I was worried about whether I could trust a book that told me there was a global flood. I felt that there must be a solution, an interpretive key that would solve this problem for me, but I couldn't see it. The obvious candidate, that Genesis literally described a local flood, was tempting to accept, but as I'll explain later, I couldn't agree with that interpretation. And all the while, the New Testament passages that seemed to be referring back to a global deluge were giving me fits.

Eventually, I resolved my concerns. I came to believe that the flood story was a hyperbolic telling of a large local flood. In the time and place of the ancient Near East, flood stories, often involving a universal flood, were a primary means by which cultures conveyed and preserved their views on important characteristics about the world around them and the divine realm. Noah's flood was the Hebrews' version of this story. God used the flood story to tell His people about sin, judgment, faith, and many other things.

Having a biblically sound understanding of the Genesis flood account that is in accord with modern science is important for me, and I believe it is important for the church as well. As with creation, I am not suggesting that Christians need to drop their traditional interpretation of the flood account. I am merely encouraging all the church to accept that a nonliteral reading of the flood story can result in a viable alternative interpretation. Having an accepted interpretation that syncs with science would comfort the hearts and minds of Christians who do not believe in a global flood and who struggle with the traditional interpretation. These Christians would not have to worry that they are disbelieving God's Word nor be tempted to think that a small piece of the Bible is not true. They could rest secure in their trust in God's Word.

Just as importantly, if not more so, a good understanding of how the Genesis flood account came to be may help us productively engage with unbelievers. The flood account is one of the sections of Scripture that opponents of the church attack most often and most vigorously. I fear that sometimes their efforts gain traction and do diminish the credibility of Christians among unbelievers. A recent experience brought this home for me.

One night I was wandering around YouTube in search of interesting or helpful videos about the flood. I was not having much luck until I came across a series by a guy with the screen name AronRa. Each video in the series takes an area of science and explains how that science disproves Noah's flood. Titles include "How Geology

Disproves Noah's Flood," "How Zoology Disproves Noah's Flood," and so forth. At this time, I was well into my research on the flood and had a good working draft of the section that argues that the YEC version of the flood—that of a global deluge that destroys all but eight people—didn't happen. So this guy's work paralleled my own in a way, although his treatment of the YEC position was more extensive than mine is. He is articulate and informed, and the videos are well done.

Mr. Ra, however, is a staunch atheist. The underlying purpose of his videos seems to be to use the flood story as a cudgel with which to attack Christianity. He does this by turning YEC arguments in favor of a global flood into insinuations that God does not exist. One of his prominent techniques is using sarcasm and ridicule to "laugh Christianity to scorn." He reminds me of a modern-day Goliath, a mighty warrior on the battlefield of apologetics, blaspheming the Lord of Hosts. Unfortunately, he appears to be making headway in using YEC arguments as tools against my church. This situation is exactly what Augustine was talking about when he warned about the dangers of Christians reading incorrect science into the Bible.[170]

Mr. Ra is using the contradictions between a concrete, literal reading of Noah's flood and our knowledge of modern science to try to keep people from Jesus. And so it is important that we have a reply ready when atheists point out the scientific problems with the literal flood narrative.

It also is useful to have ready answers to questions from unbelievers who are legitimately seeking God and are open to our faith. This is because, like a young earth doctrine, a global flood doctrine can be an impediment for potential believers. We need to do all we can to eliminate that barrier, using responsible interpretation of Scripture.

Imagine a scenario where you are sharing your faith with a young scientifically minded and well-educated colleague—let's call him Tom—over a series of Friday lunches. Tom did not grow up in a religious home, and like a large number of folks his age, he sort of believes there is a God but does not identify with a religion. And he never goes to church. You impress upon him the evidence that nature offers for the existence of God, from the majesty of the earth to the fine-tuning of the universe. So far, so good. He can see that plainly. You add that we all have a desire in our hearts for a relationship with God and an innate sense that something akin to that has been lost. Tom can sort of relate. Then you share with him that you believe that the God of the Bible is that God. You share the gospel with him, explaining that although we are all separated from God due to sin, God made a way to reunite us with Himself by sending His Son to pay the price for our sins. Tom is a bit skeptical, but open-minded. You share with Tom your own relationship with Jesus, describing what He has done in your heart and in your life. He is impressed that you would share something so personal with him, and that adds credibility to this Christianity thing in his mind. You explain to Tom some of the evidence for the life and resurrection of Jesus—for example, how the survival and spread of the early church speaks to the reality of the resurrection. You also describe how the Old Testament—written before Jesus lived and vouched for by people who do not believe that Jesus is God—prophesied about Jesus, and you explain how Jesus fulfilled those prophecies. You can see that Tom is intrigued and even a little excited. You think about inviting him to church.

Then the topic of early Genesis comes up. Tom asks you what Noah's ark—one of the few parts of the Old Testament that Tom is familiar with—was all about and how it could have happened. He doesn't believe in a global flood and doesn't want to be part of a religion that teaches things he is very sure are falsehoods.

What do you tell Tom? You need to present him with the truth of Scripture. It would be helpful if, in doing so, you do not make God's special revelation appear to be in conflict with what we know of His general revelation.

As I mentioned above, I believe that, while based upon a real local flood, the Genesis account is a grand saga employed by God to convey important theological truths. In the chapters that follow, I will trace out the path whereby I arrived at that conclusion. This path starts with the science. We will see that the flood, like creation, is an area where we should let general revelation provide us with insight into how best to interpret Scripture.

Notes

170   Augustine, *The Literal Meaning of Genesis*, trans. John Hammond Taylor, S. J. (Mahwah, NJ: Paulist, 1982), 1:42–43.

CHAPTER 22

There Was No Global Flood

The case against a global flood seems rock solid to me. I'll outline just some of the evidence that disproves a universal flood. For a more extensive treatment, you could see, for example, the work of Robert Moore,[171] Paul Seely,[172] Bruce Gordon,[173] Don Stewart,[174] or Davis Young.[175] A particularly thorough treatment of the geological arguments is given by Davis Young and Ralph Stearley.[176]

I will note that God could have solved some of the scientific dilemmas of the global flood narrative by putting all the animals on the ark into hibernation or having angels carry kangaroos to and from Australia. Our God is, after all, a God of miracles. However, the Bible does not state that He did these things. If we claim that God did them, we are reading an awful lot into the text that isn't there. It is also worth noting the old saying that when it comes to miracles, God is an economist. He doesn't flaunt His powers unnecessarily. Furthermore, and importantly, some of the many, many miracles that would be required for a global flood include miracles of covering up the evidence of prior miracles, as no compelling evidence of a global flood exists today. So I personally rule out grand supernatural acts as explanations for a global flood.

With regard to this brief outline of why a global flood did not take place, I'll group the reasons into a few broad categories. First, if there had been a universal flood with water six miles high and lasting over a year, there would be evidence of it having taken place. As Paul Seely states, "If there had been a global flood five to seven thousand years ago, there is no way all of its erosional effects and deposits would have disappeared in the interim."[177] Yet this is what we must accept in order to believe in a global flood. On the contrary, we have plenty of geological evidence against a global flood. For example, the fact that fossils have been laid down in stages, with older creatures at lower layers and more recently existing creatures in higher layers, is compelling evidence against the YEC view of a global deluge in which dinosaurs and humans perished together. Moreover, if there had been a global deluge, we would see evidence of that in the polar ice caps, but we do not. In fact, we have measurements of the composition of the Greenland ice caps going back more than 40,000 years, and at no time have they been covered by salt water.[178]

Second, the size of the ark is unrealistic. A wooden boat 450 feet long would be an engineering feat of epic proportions even in modern times, never mind thousands of years ago. As Mark Isaak discusses, "Wood is simply not strong enough to prevent separation between the joints, especially in the heavy seas that the Ark would have encountered. The longest wooden ships in modern seas are about 300 feet, and these require reinforcing with iron straps and leak so badly they must be constantly pumped."[179] The largest wooden sailing vessel ever to carry a cargo was the six-mast schooner *Wyoming*,[180] whose deck was just 330 feet long and 50 feet wide. The *Wyoming* was built in 1909 by professional shipbuilders and sank after being in service for 12 years. And although Noah had a hundred years to build his boat, even that in itself poses a problem: "By the time the job was finished, the earlier phases would be rotting away."[181]

Third, there is the problem of the water. There is not nearly enough water on, in, and above the earth to cover Mount Everest.[182] There were no massive reservoirs to burst forth. Neither was there a vast store of water in the clouds. And even if there were these things, where did the water go? Not into underground reservoirs. There was just no place for the water to recede to. And what about the mixture of salt and fresh water that would have occurred in a global flood? Noah and his family would have had no safe water to drink on the voyage, and neither would the animals. How much water could they really have brought onto the ark, and how long would it have remained fresh? And many freshwater fish (perhaps also alligators and other non-fish creatures that live in fresh water) would have died in the flood. They too would have required refuge on this ark, but did the ark have large aquariums for them? And the flood water—its depth, violence, salinity, and pressure—would have killed all plant life on the earth, including seeds. Actually, just the water pressure of a six-mile deep "ocean" would have killed most sea creatures.[183]

Fourth, there is the problem of the animals. How did they all arrive at the ark? I don't see how kangaroos could have gotten to Mesopotamia from Australia, how polar bears could have arrived from Alaska, or how penguins could have travelled from Antarctica. Also, it is hard to fathom how various species of snakes and lizards and freshwater fish that live only in South America could have made it to the ark. Once arrived, the problems only just begin. Loading the animals into the ark seems to be an impossibility. There are, by some estimates, over 8,000,000 species on earth,[184] and there would have been more species thousands of years ago. The ark was loaded in a week, in which there are 604,800 seconds. The math just doesn't work. And I can't see how Noah kept the carnivores away from the herbivores while the animals were waiting to load. And I just can't see how brontosauruses and other large dinosaurs got on the ark and into their compartments. (YEC proponents, who believe in a universal flood, also believe that humans coexisted with dinosaurs.)

Once on board, feeding and caring for this many animals poses seemingly insurmountable challenges. Elephants, for example, consume more than 300 pounds of vegetation per day. Tigers devour a large amount of fresh raw meat. Keeping supplies, both straw and meat, from spoiling over the course of a year in moist conditions would be a daunting challenge. Also, many animals have specific diets. Pandas, for example, eat only bamboo. Satisfying all the animals' dietary requirements seems far-fetched. Furthermore, caring for animals and insects that require a certain environment—hot vs. cold, for example, or dry vs. moist—poses challenges that are overwhelming to consider. Caring for water creatures (the ones that couldn't survive outside the ark) would be especially challenging. Keeping the water in their tanks as the ark was tossed to and fro by massive waves hundreds of feet high seems problematic. Removing all the animals' waste from the ship seems impossible to me. It also seems highly improbable that none of the animals died prematurely in these unsanitary conditions. And beyond premature death, the majority of animals with life spans of less than a year would have died. And most insects would have died.

Upon debarkation, the problems continue. Carnivores again would have to be kept from the herbivores. And all animals would have to find food on a barren landscape—remember, all plant and animal life died in the flood. All animals then would have to get back to their original habitats, with the attendant difficulties already discussed. Once set in their old homes again and breeding, it would be a challenge for many species to survive with such compromised, inbred gene pools.

Fifth, there is the issue of timing. YEC proponents claim that the global flood was relatively recent, perhaps about 2500 BC. Yet there were major civilizations in various parts of the world shortly before and shortly after that time. For civilizations that existed prior to 2500 BC, we have no evidence that they were wiped out by a universal flood. And for civilizations that were flourishing shortly afterward, it is unrealistic to assume that eight people repopulated the earth quickly enough to account for them. Plus, we have evidence that humans have continuously populated various parts of Mesopotamia for more than 10,000 years.[185] There is also the evidence of coral reefs, which would have been destroyed in a universal deluge yet have survived for the past hundred thousand years or more.

Every major element of the story, from the boat to the water to the animals to the timeline, seemed sufficiently problematic that I had to confirm my rejection of the idea of a global flood.

Notes

171 Robert A. Moore, "The Impossible Voyage of Noah's Ark," *Creation Evolution Journal* 4, no. 1 (1983): 1–43.

172 Paul H. Seely, "Noah's Flood: Its Date, Extent, and Divine Accommodation," *Westminster Theological Journal* 66 (2004): 291–311.

173 B. L. Gordon, "Scandal of the Evangelical Mind: A Biblical and Scientific Critique of Young-Earth Creationism," *Science, Religion and Culture* 1, no. 3 (2014): 144–73.

174 Don Stewart, "Did the Flood Cover the Entire Earth?" Blue Letter Bible, accessed September 17, 2019, https://www.blueletterbible.org/faq/don_stewart/don_stewart_667.cfm.

175 Davis A. Young, *Christianity and the Age of the Earth* (Thousand Oaks, CA: Artisan Sales, 1988).

176 Davis A. Young and Ralph F. Stearley, *The Bible, Rocks and Time* (Downers Grove, IL: InterVarsity, 2008).

177 Paul H. Seely, "Noah's Flood: Its Date, Extent, and Divine Accommodation." Seely cites Glenn Morton for the insight.

178 Paul H. Seely, "The GISP2 Ice Core: Ultimate Proof that Noah's Flood Was Not Global," *Perspectives on Science and Christian Faith* 55 (2003): 252–60.

179 Mark Isaak, "Problems with a Global Flood," The TalkOrigins Archive, last modified November 16, 1998, http://www.talkorigins.org/faqs/faq-noahs-ark.html.

180 Paul C. Morris, *American Sailing Coasters of the North Atlantic* (New York: Bonanza Books, 1979), 197.

181 Robert A. Moore, "The Impossible Voyage of Noah's Ark."

182 Bernard Ramm, *The Christian View of Science and Scripture* (Grand Rapids, MI: Eerdmans, 1954), 166.

183 Ramm, 166.

184   Richard Black, "Species count put at 8.7 million," BBC, August 23, 2011, https://www.bbc.com/news/science-environment-14616161.

185   Seely, "Noah's Flood: Its Date, Extent, and Divine Accommodation."

CHAPTER 23

....

Genesis Does Not Describe
a Local Flood

As with my effort to interpret the creation account, I began by trying to see if the flood story could be read literally. Since I had concluded there was no literal universal flood, this meant exploring whether the text might be talking about a literal flood that was local in scope. Local in scope does not mean small, of course. It just means not global. A severe local flood could certainly be large enough to inspire long-surviving oral tradition and to cause massive destruction. An event like this might not even be without precedent. Imagine how ancient cultures might have spoken of recent destructive events such as the Asian tsunami in 2004. In antiquity, with the global climate changing over time and, in particular, with ice caps melting after the last ice age, it is not unreasonable to expect that there were some really large floods. In its history, Earth has seen a number of cataclysmic events such as meteor strikes and volcanic eruptions, some of which triggered severe climate disruptions and even mass extinctions, and I presume that some of these events caused large floods. So it is reasonable to accept the possibility, or even the probability, that a particularly large flood inspired an oral tradition that later made its way into written accounts.

How does a local flood line up with Scripture? While there are good arguments to support the position that Genesis describes a local flood, arguments that may be very compelling for many readers, for me they were insufficient. I eventually moved on to examining a figurative interpretation, whereby the narrator chose to depict a local flood using global terminology. In the end I was satisfied that Scripture does not contradict our scientific knowledge with regard to the flood. But let's start with the text and then analyze the literal interpretation.

> *6:1 When man began to multiply on the face of the land and daughters were born to them, 2the sons of God saw that the daughters of man were attractive. And they took as their wives any they chose. 3Then the LORD said, "My Spirit shall not abide in man forever, for he is flesh: his days shall be 120 years." 4The Nephilim were on the earth in those days, and also afterward, when the sons of God came in to the daughters of man and they bore children to them. These were the mighty men who were of old, the men of renown."*

> *5The LORD saw that the wickedness of man was great in the earth, and that every intention of the thoughts of his heart was only evil continually. 6And the LORD regretted that he had made man on the earth, and it grieved him to his heart. 7So the LORD said, "I will blot out man whom I have created from the face of the land, man and animals and creeping things and birds of the heavens, for I am sorry that I have made them." 8But Noah found favor in the eyes of the LORD.*

> *9These are the generations of Noah. Noah was a righteous man, blameless in his generation. Noah walked with God. 10And Noah had three sons, Shem, Ham, and Japheth.*

> *11Now the earth was corrupt in God's sight, and the earth was*

filled with violence. ¹²*And God saw the earth, and behold, it was corrupt, for all flesh had corrupted their way on the earth.* ¹³*And God said to Noah, "I have determined to make an end of all flesh, for the earth is filled with violence through them. Behold, I will destroy them with the earth.* ¹⁴*Make yourself an ark of gopher wood. Make rooms in the ark, and cover it inside and out with pitch.* ¹⁵*This is how you are to make it: the length of the ark 300 cubits, its breadth 50 cubits, and its height 30 cubits.* ¹⁶*Make a roof for the ark, and finish it to a cubit above, and set the door of the ark in its side. Make it with lower, second, and third decks.* ¹⁷*For behold, I will bring a flood of waters upon the earth to destroy all flesh in which is the breath of life under heaven. Everything that is on the earth shall die.* ¹⁸*But I will establish my covenant with you, and you shall come into the ark, you, your sons, your wife, and your sons' wives with you.* ¹⁹*And of every living thing of all flesh, you shall bring two of every sort into the ark to keep them alive with you. They shall be male and female.* ²⁰*Of the birds according to their kinds, and of the animals according to their kinds, of every creeping thing of the ground, according to its kind, two of every sort shall come in to you to keep them alive.* ²¹*Also take with you every sort of food that is eaten, and store it up. It shall serve as food for you and for them."* ²²*Noah did this; he did all that God commanded him.*

^{7:1}*Then the L*ORD *said to Noah, "Go into the ark, you and all your household, for I have seen that you are righteous before me in this generation.* ²*Take with you seven pairs of all clean animals, the male and his mate, and a pair of the animals that are not clean, the male and his mate,* ³*and seven pairs of the birds of the heavens also, male and female, to keep their offspring alive on the face of all the earth.* ⁴*For in seven days I will send rain on the earth forty days and forty nights, and every*

living thing that I have made I will blot out from the face of the ground." ⁵And Noah did all that the LORD had commanded him.

⁶Noah was six hundred years old when the flood of waters came upon the earth. ⁷And Noah and his sons and his wife and his sons' wives with him went into the ark to escape the waters of the flood. ⁸Of clean animals, and of animals that are not clean, and of birds, and of everything that creeps on the ground, ⁹two and two, male and female, went into the ark with Noah, as God had commanded Noah. ¹⁰And after seven days the waters of the flood came upon the earth.

¹¹In the six hundredth year of Noah's life, in the second month, on the seventeenth day of the month, on that day all the fountains of the great deep burst forth, and the windows of the heavens were opened. ¹²And rain fell upon the earth forty days and forty nights. ¹³On the very same day Noah and his sons, Shem and Ham and Japheth, and Noah's wife and the three wives of his sons with them entered the ark, ¹⁴they and every beast, according to its kind, and all the livestock according to their kinds, and every creeping thing that creeps on the earth, according to its kind, and every bird, according to its kind, every winged creature. ¹⁵They went into the ark with Noah, two and two of all flesh in which there was the breath of life. ¹⁶And those that entered, male and female of all flesh, went in as God had commanded him. And the LORD shut him in.

¹⁷The flood continued forty days on the earth. The waters increased and bore up the ark, and it rose high above the earth. ¹⁸The waters prevailed and increased greatly on the earth, and the ark floated on the face of the waters. ¹⁹And the waters prevailed so mightily on the earth that all the high mountains under the whole heaven were covered. ²⁰The waters prevailed above the mountains, covering them fifteen cubits deep. ²¹And all flesh died that moved on the earth, birds, livestock, beasts, all swarming creatures that swarm on the earth, and all mankind. ²²Everything on the dry land in whose nostrils was the breath of life died. ²³He blotted out every living thing that was on the face of the ground, man and animals and creeping things and birds of the heavens. They were blotted out from the earth. Only Noah was left, and those who were with him in the ark. ²⁴And the waters prevailed on the earth 150 days.

⁸:¹But God remembered Noah and all the beasts and all the livestock that were with him in the ark. And God made a wind blow over the earth, and the waters subsided. ²The fountains of the deep and the windows of the heavens were closed, the rain from the heavens was restrained, ³and the waters receded from the earth continually. At the end of 150 days the waters had abated, ⁴and in the seventh month, on the seventeenth day of the month, the ark came to rest on the mountains of Ararat. ⁵And the waters continued to abate until the tenth month; in the tenth month, on the first day of the month, the tops of the mountains were seen.

⁶At the end of forty days Noah opened the window of the ark that he had made ⁷and sent forth a raven. It went to and fro until the waters were dried up from the earth. ⁸Then he sent forth a dove from him, to see if the waters had subsided from the face of the ground. ⁹But the dove found no place to set her foot, and she returned to him to the ark, for the waters were still on the face of the whole earth. So he put out his hand and took her and brought her into the ark with him. ¹⁰He waited another seven days, and again he sent forth the dove out of the ark. ¹¹And the dove came back to him in the evening, and behold, in her mouth was a freshly plucked olive leaf. So Noah knew that the waters had subsided from the earth. ¹²Then he waited another seven days and sent forth the dove, and she did not return to him anymore.

¹³In the six hundred and first year, in the first month, the first day of the month, the waters were dried from off the earth. And Noah removed the covering of the ark and looked, and behold, the face of the ground was dry. ¹⁴In the second month, on the twenty-seventh day of the month, the earth had dried out. ¹⁵Then God said to Noah, ¹⁶"Go out from the ark, you and your wife, and your sons and your sons' wives with you. ¹⁷Bring out with you every living thing that is with you of all flesh—birds and animals and every creeping thing that creeps on the earth—that they may swarm on the earth, and be fruitful and multiply on the earth." ¹⁸So Noah went out, and his sons and his wife and his sons' wives with him. ¹⁹Every beast, every creeping thing, and every bird, everything that moves on the earth, went out by families from the ark.

²⁰Then Noah built an altar to the LORD and took some of every clean animal and some of every clean bird and offered burnt offerings on the altar. ²¹And when the LORD smelled the pleasing aroma, the LORD said in his heart, "I will never again curse the ground because of man, for the intention of man's heart is evil from his youth. Neither will I ever again strike down every living creature as I have done. ²²While the earth remains, seedtime and harvest, cold and heat, summer and winter, day and night, shall not cease."

⁹:¹And God blessed Noah and his sons and said to them, "Be fruitful and multiply and fill the earth. ²The fear of you and the dread of you shall be upon every beast of the earth and upon every bird of the heavens, upon everything that creeps on the ground and all the fish of the sea. Into your hand they are delivered. ³Every moving thing that lives shall be food for you. And as I gave you the green plants, I give you everything. ⁴But you shall not eat flesh with its life, that is, its blood. ⁵And for your lifeblood I will require a reckoning: from every beast I will require it and from man. From his fellow man I will require a reckoning for the life of man. ⁶"Whoever sheds the blood of man, by man shall his blood be shed, for God made man in his own image. ⁷And you, be fruitful and multiply, increase greatly on the earth and multiply in it."

⁸Then God said to Noah and to his sons with him, ⁹"Behold, I establish my covenant with you and your offspring after you, ¹⁰and with every living creature that is with you, the birds, the livestock, and every beast of the earth with you, as many as came out of the ark; it is for every beast of the earth. ¹¹I establish my covenant with you, that never again shall all flesh be cut off by the waters of the flood, and never again shall there be a flood to destroy the earth." ¹²And God said, "This is the sign of the covenant that I make between me and you and every living creature that is with you, for all future generations: ¹³I have set my bow in the cloud, and it shall be a sign of the covenant between me and the earth. ¹⁴When I bring clouds over the earth and the bow is seen in the clouds, ¹⁵I will remember my covenant that is between me and you and every living creature of all flesh. And the waters shall never again become a flood to destroy all flesh. ¹⁶When the bow is in the clouds, I will see it and remember the everlasting covenant between God and every living creature of all flesh that is on the earth." ¹⁷God said to Noah, "This is the

CREATION AND THE FLOOD

*sign of the covenant that I have established between me and all
flesh that is on the earth."*

There are parallels between the literal local flood view and the
OEC creation view. And indeed many, perhaps most, who hold the
OEC creation view believe in a literal local flood. One commonality
between the OEC creation view and the OEC flood view is the reliance
on the small vocabulary of ancient Hebrew. The first thing I learned
with respect to the OEC flood view is that the Hebrew word that
is translated as "earth" in the passage has multiple meanings. The
word is *erets*, and while according to *Strong's Concordance* it could
mean "earth," as in the whole earth, it could also mean "land," as in a
country, territory, district, or region. As well, it could mean "ground,"
as in soil. When it is used in the Bible, erets often means land or
ground. Arthur Custance points out that "Hebrew writers evidently
employed the word with its much more restricted meaning about four
times as frequently as they employed it with a broader meaning."[186]
Custance goes on to emphasize that there is another word for earth
that is more specific, that means the whole earth. That word is *tebel*,[187]
yet the author of Genesis decided to use erets instead.

This phenomenon does not pertain only to erets. The word
translated "mountain," *har*, could also mean "hill." Translating erets as
"land" and har as "hill" radically changes the meaning of the passage.
Let's recast Genesis 7:17–20 with these new renderings: "The flood
continued forty days on the land. The waters increased and bore up
the ark, and it rose high above the land. The waters prevailed and
increased greatly on the land, and the ark floated on the face of the
waters. And the waters prevailed so mightily on the land that all the
high hills under the whole heaven were covered. The waters prevailed
above the hills, covering them fifteen cubits deep." The adjustment in
word choice certainly alters the meaning of the passage!

Furthermore, OEC proponents claim there are some verses that
could be construed as to portray a local flood. For example, in Genesis

8:11, a dove brings back an olive leaf. Olive trees do not grow on mountains, but rather on hills. So the passage may imply that the first pieces of land to reemerge from the water were the hilltops, not the mountaintops, which would never have been submerged.[188] Also, the first time Noah sent out the dove, it returned because "the waters were still on the face of the whole earth [erets]" (Genesis 8:9). But prior to this, the tops of the mountains (hills?) were seen (Genesis 8:5), implying that the erets in verse 9 signifies something more restricted than the whole globe. OEC proponents also point to Psalm 104, which is often called the creation psalm, as it praises God for His wondrous work in creating the world. Verse 9 speaks of the waters: "You set a boundary that they may not pass, so that they might not again cover the earth." OEC proponents argue that "not again" refers to Genesis 1:2, and thus Psalm 104 contradicts a global flood.

One issue I have with the OEC interpretation is that it is just not consistent with my impression of the spirit, tenor, and message of the text. Much of this is subjective, I will admit, but the text speaks in grandeur and employs universal terminology. Let's take a walk through the text and pick out some examples. Genesis 6:13 speaks of an end to all flesh, not the flesh of a particular region. And it includes humans and animals. Even if you believe that all humans were living in one region, surely animals were spread throughout the world. Genesis 6:17 could, perhaps, refer to everything within eyesight. Still, the tenor here is more significant, speaking of "all flesh in which is the breath of life under heaven." And then the repetition, to emphasize the point, that everything would die. In 7:4 God says He will kill everything He has made, not everything He made in a certain region. Genesis 7:15 is similar to 6:13, as God sure seems to be talking universally. In 7:17 the waters rise for 40 days. This doesn't sound like a local flood. Genesis 7:19 contains more epic language that is not illustrative of a local flood, even a large local flood. Likewise, 7:21–23 reads like the climactic scene in a war movie, where the camera pans out to show a silent and eerie expanse of utter and complete devastation. All flesh died.

This is big. This is grand. This is unrestrained. This is not local in any way, shape, or form. And notice the repetition here, as three times within three consecutive verses God states that everything died (except the life on the ark, of course). The destruction is complete. In 7:24 we see that the flood waters were stable at their peak for 150 days, and in 8:3 we see that they then receded for 150 days. What kind of local flood would persist for that long? Genesis 8:14 tells us the flood episode lasted longer than a year. This hardly comports with a local flood. In 8:21 God declares He will never repeat what He had just done. Yet we've had plenty of local floods since. Similarly, 9:11 says there will never be another flood like the one that He had just brought. Finally, in 9:15 God makes a covenant with the earth and with all flesh, swearing to never again do what He had just done. Is His covenant only with the people and animals of a particular region, while people and animals who now happen to live in other regions of the world are out of luck? Maybe. Again, there is subjectivity here, but to me, this story does not read like a local flood. On this score, I am in agreement with Answers in Genesis, on whose behalf Andrew Snelling and Ken Ham write, "So frequent is this use of universal terms, and so powerful are the points of comparison ("high hills," "whole heaven," and "mountains"), that it is extremely difficult to imagine what more could have been written under the direction of the Holy Spirit to express the concept of a global Flood!"[189]

Another difficulty with the OEC view is that it requires that all humankind lived within one region of the world, wherever the flood occurred. This is because the text says that all humanity died in the flood. However, this is tough to square with what we know of human history. Humanity appears to have begun in Africa and may have remained only in Africa until roughly 60,000 years ago.[190] Could the flood have occurred in Africa over 60,000 years ago? That's possible, although in that case the ark would not have ended up in Ararat. And anyway, even while humanity was still entirely contained within Africa, they as hunters and gatherers likely would have spread out farther than the scope of a local flood.

Circling back to my critique of the YEC view, the OEC view fixes some, but not all, of the deepest fundamental problems. Obviously, we don't have to worry about scientific evidence for a global flood because the OEC view does not claim a global flood. Would a local flood, big enough to be in accord with an OEC reading of the Genesis narrative, leave unambiguous, telltale traces? Perhaps. Perhaps not. And we are not sure where the flood occurred.

As for the size of the ark, that is still a problem. Many would say that the size of the ark is a bigger problem for the OEC view than it is for the YEC view because if the flood was local, why would Noah need such a large ark? And actually, why would Noah need an ark at all? Why didn't God tell Noah to travel outside the flood zone? These are fair points, but in defense of the OEC viewpoint, the ark may have been so large in that scenario to signal to us that God was open to saving all those in Noah's generation who repented. And indeed, in 2 Peter, Noah is called "a herald of righteousness" (2 Peter 2:5), implying that he preached to his neighbors as he built the ark. Still, though, the size of the ark is as much of a problem in the OEC view as it is in the YEC view. The construction of the ark, of course, remains wildly improbable. And the seaworthiness is still a problem as well, although somewhat less so, as the waters of a local flood would likely have been calmer than the waters of a global deluge.

The OEC view solves some of the problems related to water, and also the problem of timing (except for the issue of only eight humans surviving, as mentioned above). With regard to the animals, the OEC view solves some of the problems. For example, there is no need to worry about kangaroos or penguins getting to and from the ark. But other animal problems are not solved. Collecting a large number of wild animals and caring for them for a year is still quite a stretch. And the problems of keeping the carnivores away from the herbivores, both on the ark and after disembarking from it, still remain. And in addition to not solving all the problems of the animals, the OEC adds more. In particular, why did God have Noah collect all the animals in the region of the flood? Surely many of those species existed outside the flood area.

Lastly, and importantly, the New Testament authors seemed to characterize the flood as more than a local event. We'll take an in-depth look at this later.

Notes

186 Arthur C. Custance, *The Flood: Local or Global?* (Grand Rapids, MI: Academie Books, 1979), 15.

187 Custance, 16.

188 Contra this point, it could be argued that the flood covered mountains but that there were no mountains within the dove's flying radius.

189 Dr. Andrew A. Snelling and Ken Ham, "Was the Flood of Noah Global or Local in Extent?" Answers in Genesis, April 17, 2013, https://answersingenesis.org/the-flood/global/was-the-flood-of-noah-global-or-local-in-extent.

190 "Map of Human Migration," *National Geographic*, accessed September 18, 2019, https://genographic.nationalgeographic.com/human-journey.

CHAPTER 24

The Flood Story Contains Figurative Elements

With more new questions raised than answers provided, I had to drop the idea that Genesis depicts a local flood. That was disappointing. A local flood would have been an easy solution to the dilemma. Now, instead, the dilemma was getting deeper. On the one hand, I had determined that there was, in reality, no global flood. On the other hand, I had rejected the idea that the Bible depicted a local flood. In other words, there was no global flood, but the Bible depicts a global flood! Oy. This was indeed a pickle, and I didn't see a clear way out.[191]

The solution, it turns out, was simply recognizing that the flood story contains figurative elements. As I learned more and thought more about the Bible, I saw that it was common for biblical passages to contain both literal and figurative elements. For example, as Ronald L. Conte Jr. points out, "Even the expression *Love your neighbor* contains both literal and figurative elements. The term *love* is literal. The term *neighbor* is a figure, meaning that we should treat even persons who are not our neighbors as if they were."[192] I also became comfortable with my understanding that "it was common practice in the ancient world to use an event (or memory of an event) and retell it in a figurative way to communicate a message to the hearers."[193] Perhaps the most helpful thing I read was *The Lost World of the Flood* by Tremper Longman and John Walton. Eventually, the conclusion I came to was that there was a large local flood, and that Genesis portrays that flood as global in order to impart theological truths.

A Figurative Reading Solves All the Problems the YEC View Introduces

When we view the flood story through a figurative lens, the problems that are present in the YEC view fade away and disappear. To begin with, if there was no global flood, then it obviously is not a problem that we do not see any scientific evidence for a global flood. Second, the size of the ark is no longer a problem. It is fine that the literal ark was not seaworthy, because the text uses hyperbole to inflate the size of the ark. Third, the problem of the water is fixed. There would have been plenty of water available on earth to support a local flood. Fourth, the problems of the animals fade away. In a figurative reading, we do not have to believe that Noah literally took two of every animal on earth into the ark. And with a local flood, all the animals on earth would not have been wiped out. Finally, timing is no longer a concern. For example, according to a figurative reading, the flood did not literally wipe out the entire human race save eight people, and so we do not have to worry about repopulation scenarios. To summarize, a figurative reading squares completely with our scientific knowledge.

There is a lot to unpack here. First, I believe that the flood story is based on a large local flood. Basically, I don't see a reason to conclude that there was no flood disaster whatsoever. The occurrence of a particularly large flood is very plausible. Also, as we'll discuss below, the Hebrews' neighbors had flood tales as well, so there seems to have been a shared cultural memory of a cataclysmic flood event. Second, the Bible uses universal language in other places when describing local events, so it would not be unusual to see it in the story of the flood. Third, the text of the flood story offers clues that it contains figurative elements. Fourth, stories are how we learn, so it makes sense that the author of Genesis would use a story to convey his messages. And fifth, flood stories were common in the ancient Near East, and thus the flood story in Genesis served as a very effective vehicle for conveying theological truths. After discussing each of these points in turn, I'll present what I think are the most pressing theological messages from the passage. Finally, I'll show that this interpretation does not contradict other passages in the Bible that talk about the flood.

The Local Flood

It is reasonable to suppose that the Genesis flood story was based upon a real event. As we discussed before, large local floods, even catastrophic ones, do tend to happen on occasion. In the course of thousands of years prior to the writing of Genesis, I presume there was at least one in the Near East. Furthermore, various cultures in the ancient Near East seem to have a shared memory of a cataclysmic flood. Also note that melting ice caps over the period of 10,000 BC to 4000 BC were conducive to large-scale floods.

We do not know when the flood that the Genesis story is based upon occurred. The genealogies, as discussed earlier, are not reliable guides. The *Atrahasis* saga, which includes a flood account that we will discuss later, was likely composed in the third millennium BC.[194] A large catastrophic flood could have survived in oral tradition without being written down for a very long time. For instance, William Ryan and Walter Pitman tell of a volcanic eruption, the knowledge of which survived at least 1,000 years through the medium of art, specifically wall paintings.[195] It is possible that the flood occurred in 5000 or 6000 BC or even earlier.

Where did the flood occur? We don't know that either. Several sites have been proposed. One is the Black Sea. Around 5600 BC, it appears there was an enormous flood in that region. Prior to the flood, the Black Sea was a freshwater lake, cut off from the oceans by a natural dam at the Bosporus Straight. Melting polar ice caps caused the level of the Mediterranean Sea to rise to the point where it overflowed the threshold. An enormous amount of water flowed into the Black Sea. It is estimated that the flow of water was "two hundred times what flows over Niagara Falls, enough to cover Manhattan Island each day to a depth of over half a mile"; the Black Sea rose by half a foot a day, eventually rising about 330 feet.[196] Robert Ballard (who discovered the wreck of the *Titanic*), in partnership with *National Geographic*, discovered "remnants of human habitation more than 300 feet below the surface of the Black Sea, approximately 12 miles off the Turkish shore."[197] The theory of a Black Sea flood is controversial; many scientists, including those at the Woods Hole Oceanographic Institute, disagree.[198]

Another possible site for the flood is the Persian Gulf. In this scenario, the flood waters did not flow *from* the Gulf, but *into* the Gulf. The Persian Gulf itself was flooded by waters coming in from the Indian Ocean. The Gulf is quite shallow, and over the course of history, as sea levels have risen and fallen, the Gulf has been alternately wet and dry. In the last ice age, when enormous amounts of water were trapped in ice, sea levels were lower and the Gulf was dry. When it was last empty of sea water, the Gulf was an oasis. It was fed by four rivers, including the Tigris and Euphrates, and was (and still is) fed from below by large aquifers and underground springs.[199] It makes sense, then, that people would have lived there. And indeed that is just what scientists are finding. Jeffrey Rose reports "a long tradition of human occupation in the region for more than 100,000 years."[200] Indeed, "given the extent of the exposed land within the Gulf basin, the abundance of food, water, lithic raw material, and its conscripted geographic position, this sizable inland depression is thought to have formed one of the most important oases in the ancient world."[201] From around 10,000 BC, the end of the last ice age, to about 4000 BC, the Gulf filled with water from the Indian Ocean as global sea levels rose. It is likely that this process was gradual. However, it seems very plausible that an event, whether the melting of a particularly large glacier or the formation of a tsunami, could have punctuated the otherwise gradual rise with a massive and devastating flood.

There are other possible locations. Some have proposed a Caspian Sea location.[202] Furthermore, flooding in the Tigris and Euphrates river valleys are not unheard of. For example, there is evidence of a flood at current-day Fara, Iraq, the timing of which, at 2750 BC, lines up pretty well with the flood date implied by the *Sumerian King List*.[203] We will probably never know for sure. The location of the great flood has likely been lost to history.

Hyperbole and Universal Language Are Used throughout the Bible, Including in the Flood Story

We should not be surprised if we find hyperbole and universal language in the Genesis flood account because such devices are used frequently throughout the Bible. Joshua 1–12, for example, depict a complete conquest of the land of Canaan: "So Joshua took the whole land, according to all that the LORD had spoken to Moses. And Joshua gave it for an inheritance to Israel according to their tribal allotments. And the land had rest from war" (Joshua 11:23). And yet Joshua 13–24 (and Judges 1) depict a different situation: "Now Joshua was old and advanced in years, and the LORD said to him, 'You are old and advanced in years, and there remains yet very much land to possess'" (Joshua 13:1). Chapters 1 through 12 use hyperbole and universal language. They take an incomplete conquest and present it as a complete conquest. The author is not being deceitful—he gives an accurate account of the situation in chapters 13–24. Rather, he is using literary devices that the original audience would have recognized and appreciated.

For another example, compare Exodus 9:6 with 9:19. Verse 6 concerns the fifth plague, whereby God kills the livestock of the Egyptians. It uses universal language: "And the next day the LORD did this thing. All the livestock of the Egyptians died, but not one of the livestock of the people of Israel died." Yet just two plagues later, in verse 19, Moses warns Pharaoh to protect his livestock: "Now therefore send, get your livestock and all that you have in the field into safe shelter, for every man and beast that is in the field and is not brought home will die when the hail falls on them." The author of Exodus was obviously comfortable having these two verses nearly side by side because he knew that the audience would have understood the language in verse 6 to be hyperbole.

Another noteworthy example is when surrounding nations came to Joseph in Egypt to buy grain during a famine. Genesis 41:57 says, "Moreover, all the earth came to Egypt to Joseph to buy grain, because the famine was severe over all the earth." The famine affected the entire region, yet the text describes it in universal language. And this is not just an Old Testament phenomenon. See Colossians 1:23, where Paul states that the gospel "has been proclaimed in all creation under heaven." At that time, the gospel had not spread to China. These examples are just a few out of many that I could use to make my point.

The biblical authors expected the audience to understand that they were describing historical events using figurative language. And the ancient use of these literary devices was not limited to the biblical authors. As Tremper Longman and John Walton point out, "Examples in ancient literature that use universalistic language rhetorically are not difficult to find."[204] The use of hyperbole and universal language was just how writing was done back in that day. We can determine whether figurative language is being employed in a particular passage by paying careful attention to context.

When we turn our attention to the flood story, we also see these literary devices at work. We saw just recently, when looking at the text, that the tenor, tone, and language indicate a global flood. What is going on here is that the text is using hyperbole and universal language to take a local flood and describe it in global terms. So when Genesis 7:21 reports that "all flesh died that moved on the earth," that is hyperbole. So, clearly, is the size of the ark. The way the author treats the flood is similar to how the biblical authors describe the conquest of Canaan and the plagues in Egypt, except here the effect is more pronounced. With the flood story, the techniques used elsewhere in the Bible are taken to a higher level.

The flood story really is a grand epic, and the composition is exquisite. For example, the plot follows a five-stage sequence that is now the accepted "best practice" for writers of epics. Aristotle, who was born in 384 BC, wrote that an epic should "be constructed dramatically, that is, based on a single action that is whole and entire and that has a beginning, a middle, and an end" and needs "reversals."[205] At the end of the 1800s, Gustav Freytag expanded on Aristotle's comments and determined the optimal structure for an epic: "Through the two halves of the action which come closely together at one point, the drama possesses—if one may symbolize its arrangement by lines—a pyramidal structure. It rises from the *introduction* with the entrance of the exciting forces to the *climax*, and falls from here to the *catastrophe*. Between these three parts lie (the parts of) the *rise* and the *fall*."[206] Freytag was talking here about tragedies, but in modern scholarship when applied to non-tragic epics, catastrophe is simply replaced with resolution.

In the story of Noah, the introduction presents the instigating event: man has fallen into utter wickedness, epitomized by the sons of the gods cohabiting with the daughters of men. The rising action is the entrance into the ark and the rising floodwaters. We reach the climax in 8:1, when God remembers Noah, thus bringing on the reversal. The falling action is the decline of the floodwaters and the exit from the ark. Then the resolution: God blesses the whole earth.

Yet there are added layers of sophistication. The very language of the rise mirrors the language of the fall. This is called a chiastic structure. The elements of the narrative follow an A, B ... X ... B', A' pattern, where A' is the mirror or opposite of A and X is the pivot point. In the Noah story, this pattern starts at 6:9–10; A is the mention of Noah and his three sons. B is 6:11–12, the description of violence and corruption on earth. C is 6:13a, where God determines to make "an end of all flesh." And so forth through the waters prevailing upon the earth for 150 days at 7:24. The narrative pivots on the phrase, "But God remembered Noah" (8:1). The pattern starts its return journey with the waters abating for 150 days (8:3), and so forth down toward C', the commitment to preserve the earth. B' is the blessing of the earth and the covenant of peace in 9:1–17. A' is the mention of Noah and his sons in 9:18–19a. This type of device, also called a palistrophe and often presented without a pivot point, is used frequently in the Bible but perhaps nowhere as elaborately as here.

I believe the author chose to fill the opening chapters of Genesis with stories because stories are how people best learn; storytelling is the most effective way to teach a lesson. Our brains are wired for stories. Stories grab and hold our attention. Think back to high school or college, to a situation where you were struggling to pay attention or to fully grasp some material. When the teacher used a real-life or stylized example, didn't it help engage you and pull things together? This is especially helpful for visual learners. But it's not just school. It's life in general. A recent study of Super Bowl ads showed that "average consumer ratings were higher for commercials that followed a five-act dramatic form."[207] And stories don't just help with engagement and cognition; they help with retention. They provide a structure on which to hang pieces of information for storage. In preliterate times, and in the ancient Near East where the written word was not well disseminated to the average folks and oral teaching remained prevalent, this reliance on narrative was especially vital.

Perhaps most importantly, stories spur us to action. Look at effective charity campaigns. They don't just tell you the facts about the cause or endeavor for which they are raising money, but they give you real-life examples of people that will be helped by your donation. Stories even help in driving people's everyday, routine actions. A recent study showed that patients with high blood pressure adhered better to their treatment regimen when presented with stories of patients who had enjoyed successful treatment.[208] If stories work, and if God has indeed wired our brains to respond to them, it is not surprising that the biblical authors employed them.

Notes

191 Another interpretation that I explored, and rejected, was that the flood was local but the narrator thought it was global and thus depicted it as global. On various levels, this makes a good deal of sense. The account does appear to be written from the perspective of the narrator. And from where the narrator was sitting—or floating, I should say—it may have appeared like a global flood. If there was water in all directions as far as Noah could see, and if Noah could not see the nearest mountains from where he was, then he would not have known that the flood didn't cover them. Why wouldn't Noah have seen the nearest mountains? Maybe they were too far away to see. Maybe it was rainy and cloudy a lot of the time. Maybe Noah, being an old man and without modern eyeglasses, couldn't see very far. However, this interpretation does not solve, for instance, the problem of the size of the ark and some of the problems of the animals.

192 Ronald L. Conte Jr., "Noah and the Flood: literal or figurative?" *The Reproach of Christ (blog)*, January 3, 2011, https://ronconte.com/2011/01/03/noah-and-the-flood-literal-or-figurative.

193 "How should we interpret the Genesis flood account?" Biologos, accessed March 26, 2020, https://biologos.org/common-questions/how-should-we-interpret-the-genesis-flood-account.

194 Paul Tice, introduction to Albert T. Clay, *Atrahasis* (San Diego: The Book Tree, 2003).

195 William Ryan and Walter Pitman, *Noah's Flood* (New York: Simon & Schuster Paperbacks, 1998), 181.

196 Ryan and Pitman, 234–37.

197 "MIT students help uncover evidence of ancient human habitation in Black Sea," MIT News, September 20, 2000, http://news.mit.edu/2000/blacksea-0920.

198 Lonny Lippsett, "Noah's Not-so-big Flood," *Oceanus Magazine*, August 14, 2009, https://www.whoi.edu/oceanus/feature/noahs-not-so-big-flood.

199 Jeffrey I. Rose, "New Light on Human Prehistory in the Arabo-Persian Gulf Oasis," *Current Anthropology* 51, no. 6 (2010): 849–83. In particular, he writes on page 853 that "when global sea levels dropped below this mark at the onset of MIS 4, more than 100,000 km² of land were continuously exposed for the ensuing 70,000 years. During that interval, the basin housed a rich mosaic of freshwater springs, river floodplains, mangrove swamps, and estuaries."

200 Rose.

201 Rose.

202 Greg Neyman, "Where Was the Flood of Noah?" Old Earth Ministries, May 12, 2007, https://www.oldearth.org/articles/flood_location.htm.

203 P. R. S. Moorey, *Ur 'of the Chaldees'* (Ithica, NY: Cornell University Press, 1982), 34–35.

204 Tremper Longman III and John H. Walton, *The Lost World of the Flood* (Downers Grove, IL: IVP Academic, 2018), 69.

205 Aristotle, *Poetics*, trans. Anthony Kenny (Oxford: Oxford University Press, 2013), 47–48.

206 Gustav Freytag, *Freytags Technique of Drama*, trans. Elias J. MacEwan (Forgotten Books, 2012), 114–15.

207 Keith A. Quesenberry and Michael A. Coolsen, "What Makes a Super Bowl Ad Super? Five-Act Dramatic Form Affects Consumer Super Bowl Advertising Ratings," *Journal of Marketing Theory and Practice* 22, no. 4 (2014): 437–54.

208 Thomas K. Houston et al., "Culturally Appropriate Storytelling to Improve Blood Pressure: A Randomized Trial," *Annals of Internal Medicine* 154, no. 2 (2011): 77–84.

CHAPTER 25

The Power of a Story

Okay. So the passage employs figurative elements. It takes a large local flood and portrays it as a global event, in the form of an epic story, in order to effectively impart theological truths. In the ancient Near East, flood stories were particularly good vehicles for delivering truth. A primary reason is that everyone had one. Israel's northern and eastern neighbors had flood stories that predated Genesis, likely by more than 1,000 years. The great flood was an accepted part of world history.[209] The Hebrews were likely accustomed to thinking of flood stories as a vehicle for delivering deep theological truths. The similarities between these myths and Genesis are numerous and striking. So much so that it is clear that Genesis has a relationship with them. Yet as in the rival creation accounts, the many differences are where the real action is.

My view—and I'm far from alone—is that the author of Genesis employed and adapted these myths when crafting the flood narrative. The flood story was a medium that the Hebrew audience understood and could latch on to. Each ancient Near Eastern culture seems to have had their own variant of the same basic story. The sequence was always the same: creation, primeval time, flood, more time passage, and finally the contemporaneous age. The Hebrews would have expected their story to follow that same pattern. And this is indeed what we see in Genesis 1–11. We have creation, then primeval history, then the flood, then more time leading up to Abraham and the commencement of a contemporaneous history. This pattern provided a cognitive base upon which truth could be layered. And the layering is done largely through emphasis of the differences between the Genesis story and the pagan accounts. In effect, the flood story was used as a vehicle by the author of Genesis in order to highlight truths about God. And this is what we will see when we read the text of Genesis within its ancient Near Eastern context rather than from our 21st-century perspective.

Perhaps the oldest ancient Near Eastern flood story is contained within the so-called *Eridu Genesis*, a Sumerian text written in cuneiform. This comes to us from a single surviving tablet, dated to roughly 1600 BC (but the story it tells is likely much older). The tablet is missing several pieces, leaving gaps in the narrative, but it is assumed that the opening portion of the text contains a creation account. In the first section available to us, the god Nintur establishes civilization; next there is a list of pre-flood kings of Mesopotamian cities. These kings live a very long time. Indeed they do not reach adulthood until they become 100 years old. After the king list is presented, the story picks up: we witness the gods deciding to destroy the world with a great flood. "But Enki interceded by warning Ziusudra, the Sumerian flood hero, who constructed a boat and was saved from the flood. In the end, Ziusudra was rewarded with eternal life."[210] The structural similarities with Genesis are clear, as Thorkild Jacobsen points out: "Both traditions are tripartite and have in order first the creation of man and animals, second lists of leading figures after creation, in Mesopotamia city-rulers with their reigns, in the Bible, patriarchs with the years they lived, and then the flood."[211]

The epic of *Atrahasis*, written in Akkadian (from modern-day Syria) and set in the third millennium BC, was "the most popular story in the ancient world."[212] In this tale, the major gods create junior gods to do their work for them. The junior gods get tired of working, and so mankind is created to do the work, which consists of digging canals and such. The humans (who have long lifespans at this time) have children and grow plentiful. After 1,200 years, there are enough of them that they make a lot of noise. So much noise that the gods can't sleep. The gods send pestilence and drought to bring the human population down, but each time their plans are thwarted. Finally, the gods decide to send a flood to completely wipe out the humans. One of the major gods has sympathy for the humans and warns one of them, Atrahasis, in a dream. The god speaks to the wall of Atrahasis's house. Atrahasis, being on the other side of the wall, hears the god. This high god, Enki (or Ea, depending upon the version), directs Atrahasis to build a boat. The boat is a cube, and very large. Atrahasis takes skilled craftsmen with him, as well as his family and every sort of animal. The gods are "alarmed by the full force of the flood," and they "cowered like dogs from the crash of the deluge."[213] The flood lasts seven days. On the seventh day, Atrahasis releases a dove, then a swallow, and then a raven, which finds land. After the flood, Atrahasis makes a food offering for the gods, who are famished because the flood denied them the laborers who cooked for them. They gather over the offering like a swarm of flies. The high gods decide never to destroy all of humanity, but instead to keep their numbers in check by means of predators, sickness, and war. They also restrict humans' natural lifespans. A god offers a necklace of flies as a symbol of remembrance.

The Babylonian flood story is contained within *The Epic of Gilgamesh* and seems to be adapted from *Atrahasis*. In *The Epic of Gilgamesh*, the gods decide to exterminate mankind. The god Ea warns the flood hero, Upnapishtim, of the pending deluge. Ea instructs Upnapishtim to tear down his reed-house and use the reeds to make a boat, and to take on the boat "the seed of all living creatures."[214] The ark is built in seven days, and Upnapishtim loads into the boat all his wealth, his family, wild and tame animals, and craftsmen of all types. The gods are terrified at the flood. They "crouched against the walls, cowering like curs."[215] On the seventh day of the flood, the waters subside and the boat rests on a mountain. After seven more days, Upnapishtim releases a dove, then a swallow, and then a raven. The passengers disembark and make a sacrifice. The gods, as in *Atrahasis*, swarm over the sacrifice. The gods regret the flood. A goddess lifts a necklace of jewels in remembrance. Upnapishtim and his wife are blessed and are granted eternal life.

In Genesis and in these pagan myths, God or gods decide to wipe out humanity with a flood. God or gods warn one man. That man builds a boat and saves himself, his family, and animals. The man lets out birds. He offers a sacrifice. The sacrifice is accepted. This is just a partial list of the similarities, and already there are too many conspicuous similarities to be a coincidence. But there are loads of differences as well. Genesis has one God, versus many gods in the pagan stories. In Genesis, God, who is the protagonist of the story, is decisive. In the pagan stories, the many gods bicker about what to do and are not unified. In Genesis, God punishes wickedness. In the pagan stories, the gods are annoyed that man was making too much noise. In Genesis, God is in control of the flood. In the pagan stories, the flood gets out of control and scares the gods. In Genesis, God accepts the sacrifice but does not need it. In the pagan stories, the gods desperately need the food. In Genesis, God blesses humanity, tells us to be fruitful and multiply, and promises never to again destroy the world with a flood. In the pagan stories, a god promises to remember the event, and the gods resolve to find other ways to keep the human population under control.

So what gives? As I mentioned, I believe that the author of Genesis used the structure of the flood story as a vehicle to present deep theological truths. To explore those truths, we will make our way through the flood story, following the path of Freytag's pyramid.

Notes

209 W.G. Lambert and A.R. Millard, *Atra-hasis* (Winona Lake, IN: Eisenbrauns, 1999), 18.

210 Kenton L. Sparks, *Ancient Texts for the Study of the Hebrew Bible* (Grand Rapids, MI: Baker, 2017), 311.

211 Thorkild Jacobsen, "The Eridu Genesis," *Journal of Biblical Literature* 100, no. 4 (1981): 513–29.

212 Paul Tice, introduction to Albert T. Clay, *Atrahasis* (San Diego: The Book Tree, 2003).

213 Timothy J. Stephany, *Enuma Elish* (United States: Createspace, 2014), 100.

214 N.K. Sandars, *The Epic of Gilgamesh* (London: The Penguin Group, 1972), 108.

215 Sandars, 110.

CHAPTER 26

....

Introduction and
Instigating Event

The introduction to the flood story is found in Genesis 6:1–8. The first four verses in particular present the instigating event and serve as one of the most difficult passages in the Bible to interpret. But everybody likes a mystery, so it gets lots of attention. And since it is at the headwaters of the flood story, we need to address it. I've reprinted the introduction here for easy reference.

> *6:1 When man began to multiply on the face of the land and daughters were born to them, 2 the sons of God saw that the daughters of man were attractive. And they took as their wives any they chose. 3 Then the LORD said, "My Spirit shall not abide in man forever, for he is flesh: his days shall be 120 years." 4 The Nephilim were on the earth in those days, and also afterward, when the sons of God came in to the daughters of man and they bore children to them. These were the mighty men who were of old, the men of renown.*
>
> *5 The Lord saw that the wickedness of man was great in the earth, and that every intention of the thoughts of his heart was*

*only evil continually. ⁶And the Lord regretted that he had made man on the earth, and it grieved him to his heart. ⁷So the L*ᴏʀᴅ *said, "I will blot out man whom I have created from the face of the land, man and animals and creeping things and birds of the heavens, for I am sorry that I have made them." ⁸But Noah found favor in the eyes of the L*ᴏʀᴅ.

Regarding the first four verses, there are three leading interpretations out there. All have significant difficulties but strengths as well. First, the majority view, which I'll call the "angels" view, supposes that the "sons of God" are fallen angels that have cohabited with human women. Rendering "sons of God" as angels, like in Job 2:1, seems to be the most natural surface reading. Proponents of this view take the Nephilim to be the offspring of the angels and women. Angels mating with humans is abhorrent to God and contributes to God's decision to wipe out His creation and start over. On the surface it may seem unfair to blame humanity for the transgressions of angels, but these unions may have been entered into willingly by the women (and their fathers, who in a patriarchal society would have given final authority and blessing). Indeed, a possible motive for the humans was to extend the lifespans of their progeny.²¹⁶ And more than extending lifespans, mating with angels may also have been an attempt to "cross the boundary between themselves and God," which could have been "the final straw which led to God's decision to destroy the world."²¹⁷

We see angels take human form elsewhere in the Bible (e.g. Genesis 18–19), but can they cohabit with humans? If they can take human form, I don't see why not. Jesus says that in heaven angels don't marry—"For in the resurrection they neither marry nor are given in marriage, but are like angels in heaven" (Matthew 22:30)—but does not comment about what fallen angels on earth might do. Would such a union produce children? I suppose that could happen. Would that alter the human gene pool, such that we would be able to detect those children's genes in our current gene pool? Perhaps not, especially if the angels indwelt particular human hosts without changing their DNA. Yet the passage alludes to a physical change, saying the offspring lived longer lives and became "mighty men." Anyway, this interpretation was prevalent back in the days of the early church. The First Book of Enoch, or 1 Enoch, was an apocryphal book from the second century BC that advanced this traditional interpretation. First Enoch influenced the biblical writers but was not ultimately selected for inclusion in the Bible. Jude is likely referencing 1 Enoch's interpretation of Genesis 6:1–4 when he writes, "And the angels who did not stay within their own position of authority, but left their proper dwelling, he has kept in eternal chains under gloomy darkness until the judgment of the great day" (Jude 1:6). Similarly, 2 Peter 2:4 may be referring to God's judgment on the sons of God: "For if God did not spare angels when they sinned, but cast them into hell and committed them to chains of gloomy darkness to be kept until the judgment." So might 1 Peter 3:19, which says Jesus "went and proclaimed to the spirits in prison." But *may* and *might* are the key words here.

Another common theory is that "sons of God" instead refers to men of the line of Seth who married women from the line of Cain. I'll call this the "Sethite" view. This interpretation fits very well with the flow and themes of Genesis. As we discussed earlier, Genesis 5 traces the lines of Seth and Cain, highlighting the godliness of Seth's line and the ungodliness of Cain's line. The next logical step in that progression is the two lines intermarrying. That, in turn, provides background and explanation for how evil and corruption infected the whole human race in Genesis 6:5–8. God's anger at the godly men of the line of Seth marrying into the ungodly line of Cain foreshadows God's later warnings to the Israelites not to marry Canaanites; such intermarriages would lead to the Israelites taking on the idolatrous worship and sinful practices of the Canaanites. In a similar way, the mixing of the line of Seth with the line of Cain, which was known for violence and sin, may have led to the moral degeneration of the Sethites. As Paul writes in 1 Corinthians 15:33, "Bad company ruins good morals." The flood goes on to completely wipe out the line of Cain. But what about the Nephilim? Well, a careful reading of the text shows that it does not explicitly state that the Nephilim are the offspring of the sons of God and the daughters of men. The text could be read to say that the Nephilim were contemporaries of the men of the line of Seth.

Another theory, not as common as the other two, is that the "sons of God" should be translated "sons of the gods," small *s* and small *g*. They are earthly royalty, and I'll call this the "kings" view. I think this view has a lot to commend it, and I prefer it to the other two. It fits the text quite well, even the obscure details that have flummoxed readers. Also, it fits with the wider pattern of early Genesis being in conversation with ancient Near Eastern culture. Let's take the passage verse by verse.

In verse 1, the action starts by focusing on a population increase. This is typical among other ancient Near Eastern flood traditions: an increase in population sets off a chain of events culminating in the flood. For example in *Atrahasis* the text reads, "Twelve hundred years had not yet passed when the land extended and the peoples multiplied. The land was bellowing like a bull, the god got disturbed with their uproar."[218] So right away we see that Genesis is adapting ancient Near Eastern cultural themes.

Moving on to verse 2, in this interpretation the sons of god are earthly kings like Gilgamesh, who was likely a real person and is accounted for in the *Sumerian King List*.[219] The earthly kings were often said to have been the offspring of gods and humans, and the kingships of the cities were granted by the gods. So the earthly kings were considered to be, literally, sons of the gods. For example, Gilgamesh was said to be two-thirds divine and one-third human. Claiming to be deity is a big no-no in the Lord's eyes. Continuing along in verse 2, the earthly kings engaged in the deplorable practice of taking any woman they chose. In *The Epic of Gilgamesh*, it is said that "Gilgamesh the king is about to celebrate marriage with the Queen of Love, and he still demands to be first with the bride, the king to be first and the husband to follow, for that was ordained by the gods from his birth, from the time the umbilical cord was cut. … His lust leaves no virgin to her lover, neither the warrior's daughter nor the wife of the noble."[220] It seems that in the ancient Near Eastern culture, the kings would sleep with brides on their wedding night. Also, we know that those cultures practiced cult prostitution and sacred marriage, a fertility right involving sexual union between a god (represented by a priest) and a human, "upon which the annual fertility of the land was believed to depend."[221] Genesis could well be commenting on the wickedness of these practices, which are also likely a microcosm of all the evil deeds going on at the time, and which in turn explains well why God decided to wipe the slate clean.

Verse 3 has spawned a good deal of controversy. Many scholars believe that God is saying that He will give humanity 120 years and then wipe them out. It is interesting that in *Atrahasis*, the period between each of a set of pre-flood catastrophes that were supposed to wipe out humans is 1,200 years,[222] which is 120 times 10. So again, it seems Genesis is making its point in connection with the ancient Near Eastern traditions.

Moving on to verse 4, the Nephilim fit nicely into this interpretation; perhaps the Nephilim were the offspring of the kings. Many scholars are confused by the phrase "and also afterward," which doesn't make much sense in the angel and Sethite interpretations; how could the Nephilim survive the flood? But this is easily explained within the kings interpretation. The *Sumerian King List* shows kings both before and after the flood. The text seems to be acknowledging that the Nephilim, the children of these kings, would have been around as a class both before and after the flood.[223]

Is this interpretation contradicted by the New Testament passages mentioned above under our discussion of the angel interpretation? In other words, do the New Testament passages cited support the angel theory and exclude the kings theory? I don't think so. Besides, the New

Testament authors may merely be giving an additional meaning to the passage, which would help explain why it is so difficult to interpret. For example, as Waltke argues, the truth could be a combination of the kings and angels views, with the kings being possessed by demons.[224] I agree with Waltke that the two theories need not be mutually exclusive. For that matter, I don't think the Sethite theory is mutually exclusive either. Sethite men could have married women from the line of Cain and become corrupted by the growing culture of violence. Earthly kings could have been behaving badly. Fallen angels could have been behaving badly. These three things could all have been happening at once, especially when the entire world was going down the tubes ethically. This takes us to verse 5.

Verse 5 indicates that wickedness was pervasive on the earth. I take it that the incidents alluded to in verse 2 were just a flagship example of what was going on throughout humanity. Verse 11 seems to indicate this as well, as it says the earth was filled with violence. Verse 6 relates that this wickedness caused God to regret creating the world, and in verse 7 He resolves to wipe out all living things. Verse 8 introduces Noah into the story.

One noteworthy feature of the Genesis story is that God is the central character. Noah does not even speak. God is the protagonist. His created world is falling apart, and He determines to destroy it. But the introduction hints at God bestowing grace through Noah, who found favor in His eyes.

Man Is Wicked

One clear lesson from this text is that humans are wicked. We are full of sin. The sin proceeds from, is a result of, our fundamental character, which is corrupt. Notice verse 5. Man is wicked, and the innermost part of his being is constantly producing evil. This is human nature.

This is who we are at our core. The text does not mince words: our nature is flat-out rotten. We are in constant rebellion against God. And notice I said this is who we *are*, not who we *were*. The text is telling a story of antiquity, but it is clearly also speaking about us today. After the flood, when speaking about the future of the human race, God says in Genesis 8:21 that "the intention of man's heart is evil from his youth." And this message is repeated throughout the Bible. As David Platt emphasizes, "The biblical gospel says, 'You are an enemy of God, dead in your sin.'"[225] So, after the flood we are just as corrupt in our core as we were before the flood. And this makes perfect sense. After all, how could the flood change our innermost character? How did the flood alter human nature? It couldn't, and it didn't. Our nature is deeply, completely corrupt, and as a result we are thoroughly sinful. The Psalms were written in a post-flood world, yet the psalmist relates, "There is none who does good, not even one" (Psalm 53:3; see also Psalm 14:3). Similarly, Isaiah prophesies, "All we like sheep have gone astray; we have turned—every one—to his own way" (Isaiah 53:6).

Not only are we personally as corrupt as the people described in Genesis 6, but our world is steeped in sin just as the pre-flood world was. In my own country, our practice of slavery only ended about 150 years ago. Globally, episodes of massive genocide in the 20th and 21st centuries have been common enough to engender little or no surprise. Stalin and Hitler each killed several million people. Pol Pot in Cambodia wiped out perhaps a quarter of his population. Ethnic cleansing campaigns were waged in the Balkans. In the space of a year, close to a million Tutsis were slaughtered in Rwanda. Hundreds of thousands were murdered in Darfur. In the Middle East, children are used as human shields. Throughout the world, acts of terrorism seem commonplace. The most prominent example is 9/11, but more recently al-Qaeda has targeted schoolgirls in Afghanistan, as has Boko Haram in Nigeria. ISIS has emerged as the leading global terrorist group, gaining volunteers and support because they are *more* brutal than al-Qaeda. Wars of choice, based upon greed, power, or raw hatred, fill the world. In recent years, Syria and Yemen have been utterly obliterated by war. Sex slavery and child prostitution are rampant across the world. Recently, a large and longstanding child sexual exploitation ring was uncovered in England, one of the most civilized nations in the world. I could, of course, go on for a long time. And these examples that I've highlighted are just outward manifestations of the world's deep inner corruption.

The world is deeply corrupt because each of us as individuals is corrupt. Sure, most of us are not like Pol Pot, but we are from the same stock. We are all sinners. Indeed, "if we say we have no sin, we deceive ourselves, and the truth is not in us" (1 John 1:8). Because we are sinners, we are not qualified to condemn anyone else. As the apostle James writes, "There is only one lawgiver and judge, he who is able to save and to destroy. But who are you to judge your neighbor?" (James 4:12).

God Judges Sin

There is one "righteous judge" (2 Timothy 4:8), and judge He does. Another lesson from the text is that sin is serious, and God judges sin. The pervasive wickedness in 6:5, represented by the actions of 6:2, causes God to commit to destroy the world. And here we have to step back a moment and delve into some things that are implicit, but not directly stated, within this particular passage. There is an elephant in the room. As Christians, we proclaim that we have a loving God. And yet the passage says that God ... killed ... every ... person ... on ... the ... earth—except for eight. And if Noah had not found favor in God's eyes, He would have obliterated every living creature on the planet. We have a wrathful God. And this is a barrier for many in accepting Christianity. Why is God wrathful, and how can He be loving if He judges so harshly?

We can't brush this aside as some sort of isolated event in the Bible. It is not. The Old Testament in particular is chock-full of instances of God harshly punishing people who sin and of passages where God condemns sin. "Fourteen times in the first fifty psalms alone, we are told that God hates the sinner, his wrath is on the liar, and so forth."[226] And the New Testament is full of warnings of eternal damnation. Perhaps the most challenging thing, however, is that several times in the Bible God severely punishes those who, in our eyes, do things that aren't really that bad. One example of this relates to Moses. Now, Moses and God are tight. They have a great relationship. Yet God deals firmly with Moses. In Numbers 20, while wandering in the wilderness, the Hebrews lose their water source. God instructs Moses to speak to a rock and have water flow forth from the rock. Moses brings forth water from the rock, but with his words he implicitly attributes authority, credit, and honor to himself for the miracle rather than making it clear that God is acting on His own to perform this miracle. Also, rather than speaking to the rock as God instructs, Moses strikes it with his staff. As a result of this incident, God denies Moses entry into the Promised Land; he eventually dies on the east side of the Jordan River. This certainly appears harsh to our modern sensibilities.

Another example is from the story of Uzzah and the ark (2 Samuel 6:1–7; 1 Chronicles 13:9–10). The Israelites are transporting the ark of the covenant. They put it on a cart rather than carrying it with poles as they are supposed to do (again, disrespecting God). The ox that is pulling the cart stumbles, and the ark starts to tip. Fearing that the ark will fall off the cart, and in concern for the safety of the ark, Uzzah reaches out his hand and touches the ark to stabilize it. The problem is, Uzzah is not allowed to touch the ark. Numbers 4:15 prescribed the death penalty for such an offense. And so, as punishment for touching the ark and disobeying Him, God immediately strikes Uzzah dead. Just for trying to keep the ark from falling! Another classic example is Lot's wife. In Genesis 19, God saves Lot and his family from the destruction of Sodom and Gomorrah but tells them not to look back as they flee the city. Yet as they are walking from Sodom a safe distance away, while the city is being consumed with fire from the sky, Lot's wife looks back, disobeying God (see a pattern here?). The temptation was great. How often do you see the Lord raining sulfur and fire upon a city? And the offense seemed small—just a peek. And yet the consequence was severe. Lot's wife turned into a pillar of salt.

Another striking example comes from the New Testament. Very early in the church, the believers were living together and sharing everything in common. The rule was if you sold property—which wasn't a requirement, but if you did—then you had to give the proceeds to the community, which would then distribute it to any who had need. In Acts 5, we have the story of Ananias and his wife Sapphira. They sell some property but only give part of the proceeds to the church. And they lie about it, telling Peter that they contributed the whole amount. As a result, God strikes them dead. On the spot. My family and I recently watched a video about the importance of truthfulness that featured a reenactment of the story of Ananias and Sapphira. When Ananias fell dead, there was a moment of still silence in our family room (a conspicuous rarity in our family room). Then there were exclamations of shock and disagreement from our kids. Jonathan exclaimed, "Wait, what?! He died?!" "That's not fair!" came from Isabel. Gasps emanated from Clare and Sam. And I understand what my kids were getting at. Sure, Ananias and Sapphira sinned. They lied. But a death sentence? To call it a severe punishment is an understatement.

God's Authority and Holiness

If we are shocked by God's actions, that signals that we, somehow, are not looking at God from the proper perspective. Here, I think there are two things going on. We do not have sufficient respect for God's authority, and we do not have full appreciation of His holiness. Our

American church culture deemphasizes these, let alone our secular culture. When my kids reacted as they did to the story of Ananias and Sapphira, I told them that when I was growing up, I heard a saying that has stuck with me: "Don't mess with the bull, or you'll get the horns." Now, that analogy is flawed in several respects—I was put on the spot, just doing my best in the moment—and I followed up with the standard encouragement to take sin, including and perhaps especially lying, very seriously. But what I was trying to emphasize with my aphorism was God's authority and His ability to project that authority. Our God is not the Pillsbury Doughboy. He is the almighty ruler of the universe. He is not to be messed with, dishonored, or disrespected. And because of His supreme authority, the consequences may justifiably be large. If there weren't consequences, His authority would be diminished. Don't play with God.

It is said in Proverbs 9:10 that "the fear of the LORD is the beginning of wisdom." We are often told that the word "fear" in this context should be understood as "awe" rather than as being afraid. But in some sense, even a secondary sense, should it not also involve actual raw fear? God brought us into this world, and God can take us out. And He can (and will) put us in hell if we are not (or do not become) believers. Matthew 10:28 says, "And do not fear those who kill the body but cannot kill the soul. Rather fear him who can destroy both soul and body in hell." I used to think that referred to Satan, but I now understand it to refer to God. And indeed it is perhaps more explicit in Luke 12:5, which says, "But I will warn you whom to fear: fear him who, after he has killed, has authority to cast into hell. Yes, I tell you, fear him!" It is God who has the authority to send people to hell, although in a real sense we send ourselves to hell by not accepting God's free gift of salvation. "Whoever does not believe is condemned already, because he has not believed in the name of the only Son of God" (John 3:18).

Once we are saved, we no longer need to fear hell. However, we should be wary of discipline. As we saw above, just as God denied

Moses entry into the Promised Land, He dishes out consequences even to those with whom He has a tight relationship. Furthermore, Hebrews 12:10 tells us that God "disciplines us for our good," and Augustine writes, "O Lord, for you teach us by inflicting pain."[227] Yes, when we are disciplined by God, we should embrace that discipline and submit to it. But I, for one, would rather get my heart and actions right with God so that I don't require His discipline as often!

The other element of God that we fail to adequately appreciate is His holiness. His pure, white-hot, all-consuming holiness. This holiness is a part of His character, and as a result it must be protected always. Sin in the presence of God is an offense to His holiness. If sin were allowed to dwell with God, He would not be holy. The holiness of God is illustrated in Isaiah 6, in which Isaiah has a vision. The Lord is sitting on a throne, and six seraphim are above Him. Each has six wings, and two of the wings cover their faces. God's glory is so great that they cannot even stand to look at Him. In verse 3, one calls to another, "Holy, holy, holy is the LORD of hosts; the whole earth is full of his glory!" As R.C. Sproul explains, "On a handful of occasions the Bible repeats something to the third degree. To mention something three times in succession is to elevate it to the superlative degree, to attach to it emphasis of superimportance."[228] Holiness is an integral part of God's glory. Isaiah himself sees the Lord and worries that he will perish because he, a sinner, cannot be in the presence of such holiness and live. Holiness and sin cannot coexist. In verse 5 he says, "Woe is me! For I am lost; for I am a man of unclean lips, and I dwell in the midst of a people of unclean lips; for my eyes have seen the King, the LORD of hosts!" One of the seraphim purifies Isaiah's lips with a burning coal, and his sin is atoned for.

Another illustration of God's holiness occurs in Exodus 33. Moses asks to see God's glory. God responds graciously that He will pass by Moses, but warns Moses in verse 20 that "you cannot see my face, for man shall not see me and live." God is so holy that man cannot look upon Him and live. So God puts Moses in a cleft of a rock, and as He passes by Moses, God covers Moses's face with His hand. Thereby Moses is protected from seeing God's face.

Sin, then, impugns God's character. It is an assault on His holiness and on His authority. It must be repaid to protect God's holiness and authority. Wrath is not a part of God's intrinsic character. God's character involves things that are always true about Him. Like love. God always loves, continually, in every circumstance. Although it seems a distinction without a difference as we are always sinning, there is no wrath from God apart from sin. Wrath is merely a rational response to sin's assault on God's character. So yes, God hates sin and sends His wrath on sinners. And since we sin continually—see Genesis 6:5 again—God's wrath is continually on unbelievers. Note John 3:36, where Jesus says that "whoever does not obey the Son shall not see life, but the wrath of God remains on him." Jesus says "remains." The wrath of God had been on all people since the fall. After the cross, the wrath of God only remains on unbelievers.

For believers, whose sins have been paid for and who are now "white as snow" (Isaiah 1:18), God's holiness has turned from something to fear into a source of great joy. This sank in for me while watching a Paul Washer sermon.[229] As the apostle Paul says in Romans 5:1, "Since we have been justified by faith, we have peace with God through our Lord Jesus Christ." Furthermore, John quotes Jesus as saying, "Truly, truly, I say to you, whoever hears my word and believes him who sent me has eternal life. He does not come into judgment, but has passed from death to life" (John 5:24). And once we have eternal life, we cannot lose it: Jesus goes on to say that "all that the Father gives me will come to me, and whoever comes to me I will never cast out" (John 6:37). In the context of this reality, God's holiness means that if we are in Him, He will never mistreat us. We can trust that He, now and forevermore, is "for us" (Romans 8:31). The Father, who sent His Son to die for our sins, will always treat us with love. His holiness ensures it.

As I noted, love is also part of God's character. First John 4:8 states that "anyone who does not love does not know God, because God is love." And John 3:16 tells us that "God so loved the world, that he gave his only Son, that whoever believes in him should not perish but have eternal life." And God doesn't just love believers. It is His nature, His character, to love all of us. Romans 5:8 emphasizes this when Paul says, "But God shows his love for us in that while we were still sinners, Christ died for us." In each of our salvation journeys, while we were sinners apart from God, God pursued us. He loved us first. Going back to 1 John 4, in verse 19 John explains that "we love because he first loved us."

So unbelievers experience God's wrath and His love, both at the same time. How is that possible? How can God display love and wrath simultaneously? They are tied together through justice, which like love is also part of God's character. Our God is a God of love but also a God of justice.

Divine Justice

God's justice is also severely underappreciated in our culture. For example, many say that it is not just for God to put people in hell—especially those who haven't done anything really bad. But no innocent person is punished by God, because no one is innocent. On the contrary, we all deserve hell, and it is only due to God's mercy that we are not all there right now. We were created by a loving, holy God to represent Him on this earth, and instead of obeying Him, we are in constant rebellion.

We all sin, every day. In Matthew 5 Jesus teaches that the Ten Commandments are not merely a list of big "can't do's" but are also a template for how to spot sin in our daily lives. In reflecting on the commandment against murder, Jesus emphasizes that "everyone who is angry with his brother will be liable to judgment" (Matthew 5:22). And teaching on the commandment against adultery, He insists that "everyone who looks at a woman with lustful intent has already committed adultery with her in his heart" (Matthew 5:28). From our inadequate human viewpoint, we may not consider our sins to be serious, but they separate us from God and are thus quite serious in God's eyes.

So yes, it is just for God to judge. Humanity deserves to be wiped out. The flood was just. It was not more than we deserved. We are wicked, in constant rebellion against God, and our sin is an affront to His authority and to His holiness.

Yet God's love is constant and perfect. He loves unbelievers and wants them to repent and accept His free gift of salvation. But due to His justice, every sin has to have a consequence. His authority and holiness require it. Every sin has to be paid for. Let's say I love you (as I should), and you steal cash from me. Well, although I love you, the debt has to be paid. You can pay off the debt by returning the cash. Or I can forgive the debt. In that case, the debt is still paid off, it is just that I paid it myself on your behalf. This is what Jesus did on the cross. Due to our sin, we could not be in the presence of God. We were condemned to spend eternity apart from God. But Jesus paid our debt for us so that we can be with Him in eternity.

More Lessons from the Introduction

So far we've learned from the introduction to the flood story that man is sinful and that sin is serious. We also have seen that God justly judges us and punishes sin. Humanity deserves to be wiped out, and God determines to do so in Genesis 6:7. Our God is a just God. Justice is part of His character. As we've discussed, offenses against God will not go unpaid. For unbelievers, the debt will be paid through an eternity away from God; for believers, the debt was paid by Christ at the cross.

If man is so wicked that God resolved to wipe us out, that leads us to another conclusion: The gulf between us and God is wide. Really wide. Too wide for us to bridge. And from that follows a further conclusion, which is that we need a savior. And since the savior can't be one of us, as we are unable to be our own bridge to God, the savior has to be God Himself. We need God to lay down a bridge between Him and us. And He did, via Jesus and the cross. And Jesus has come across that bridge via the incarnation and welcomes us to set foot on the bridge ourselves. We have only to take the first step onto it, and He will guide us the rest of the way.

One other point merits attention before we turn to the next chapter. God resolved, in verse 7, to wipe out all animal life. But animals are innocent. They don't sin against God. How does this square with a just God? As God's representatives who are charged to have dominion over the animals, our leadership role on earth makes us responsible for the animal kingdom. As we represent them, animals can suffer due to our sins. As Paul says in Romans 8:22, "For we know that the whole creation has been groaning together in the pains of childbirth until now." Leaders can act as representatives for others; people can be blessed or not based upon the actions of their leaders.

Notes

216 Claus Westermann, *Genesis 1–11*, A Continental Commentary (Minneapolis: Fortress, 1994), 376.

217 Andre van Oudtshoorn, "Mything the Point: The Use of Mythology in Genesis 1–11," Crucible Theology & Ministry, November 2015, https://www.academia.edu/33993693/Mything_the_Point_The_Use_of_Mythology_in_Genesis_1-11.

218 W.G. Lambert and A.R. Millard, *Atra-hasis* (Winona Lake, IN: Eisenbrauns, 1999), 73.

219 George F. Isham, *Bible Chronology and the Sumerian King List* (self-pub., 2014), 61.

220 N.K. Sandars, *The Epic of Gilgamesh* (London: The Penguin Group, 1972), 62, 68.

221 P. R. S. Moorey, *Ur 'of the Chaldees'* (Ithica, NY: Cornell University Press, 1982), 88.

222 Lambert and Millard, *Atra-hasis*, 73.

223 The Nephilim are mentioned one other time in the Bible, in Numbers 13. Unfortunately, that passage is not very helpful to our current discussion. Moses sends twelve men to spy on the land of Canaan in preparation for entering and conquering it. Upon returning, two of the spies, Joshua and Caleb, encourage the people to occupy the land. The other ten, however, "brought to the people of Israel a bad report of the land" (verse 32), claiming that the inhabitants were "stronger than we are" (verse 31); they go on to report that "there we saw the Nephilim (the sons of Anak, who come from the Nephilim), and we seemed to ourselves like grasshoppers, and so we seemed to them" (verse 33). It seems the ten spies, who were not trusting in the promises of the Lord, were behaving cowardly. The allusion to grasshoppers may indicate an exaggeration. It is also unclear whether "bad report" means unfavorable or inaccurate. In support of the report being inaccurate or an exaggeration, there are no reports of Israel encountering any actual Nephilim when they eventually occupy Canaan.

224 Bruce K. Waltke, *Genesis* (Grand Rapids, MI: Zondervan Academic, 2001), 117.

225 David Platt, *Radical* (New York: Multnomah Books, 2010), 32.

226 D. A. Carson, *The Difficult Doctrine of the Love of God* (Wheaton, IL: Crossway Books, 2000), 69.

227 Augustine, *Confessions* (London: Penguin Books, 1961), 44.

228 R.C. Sproul, *The Holiness of God* (Carol Stream, IL: Tyndale House, 1998), 24.

229 Paul Washer, "Four Pillars of Walking with God - Paul Washer," I'll Be Honest, YouTube video, December 2, 2015, https://youtu.be/7gVDRhzE8nw. The relevant portion begins at 12:45.

CHAPTER 27

Rising Action

Genesis 6:9–7:24 constitutes the rising action of the story, according to the pattern of Freytag's Pyramid. God tells Noah that He will destroy the earth with a flood, then instructs Noah to build the ark and to load it with animals and with food. God promises protection for Noah, and this promise is associated with a covenant. Noah enters the ark, and the Lord shuts him in. The flood commences, the waters rise for 40 days, and everything on land is obliterated.

God's sovereign control and immense power really jump out of the text. See 7:11, where God causes the fountains of the great deep to burst forth and opens the windows of heaven. The great deep is the sea under the earth. The windows of heaven are opened to let in the cosmic sea, which is above the firmament. Flooding the entire earth shows complete and total command of the world and evinces God's might. It also displays His sovereignty, as He did not have to consult with anyone. If the power and sovereignty displayed by God in the flood remind you of the creation account, it should. As many commentators have emphasized, the flood episode is a story of uncreation, wherein God reverses His work of creation, returning the earth to the watery formless void that existed in Genesis 1:2. It is likely that the author intended the story to be read this way. For example, notice how the opening of the windows in the firmament reverses

God's work from day two of creation when He separated the waters above the firmament from the waters below.

Faith and Obedience

During this rising action segment of the story, God instructs Noah to build a boat so that Noah and his family will survive the flood. Why did Noah find favor in God's eyes? Noah displayed faith and obedience. The text says Noah was righteous, blameless in his generation, and that he walked with God. I don't think this means that Noah was perfect and sinless. Only Jesus was sinless. And the Hebrew word *tamiym*, translated into English as "blameless," does not mean perfect or sinless. According to *Strong's Concordance* it means complete, whole, entire, sound. Besides, we see that Noah sinned after the flood, drinking to excess and ending up naked and unconscious (9:21). But Noah didn't participate in the corrupt practices of his peers. In this way he was blameless in his generation. Noah was complete and whole, acting righteously in the midst of a corrupt generation.

Noah acted righteously as a result of his walk with God. Yet walking with God starts with faith. Walking with God first and foremost implies a tight relationship with Him. Noah knew God and loved God. And God knew and loved Noah. And so Noah could walk alongside God as a friend. But our friendship with God is not like our friendships with other people. When you are friends with God, you walk alongside God and in lockstep with God, with God choosing the path. You are both alongside God and following God. Walking with God, then, implies two things: faith and obedience. Perhaps one way to put it is that faith allows you to begin to walk with Him (or resume walking with Him), and obedience allows you to remain walking with Him, to remain in lockstep with Him.

Noah's faith is legendary. Just think about the faith required to build a boat in anticipation of a flood! This is rock-solid trust in God. And so Noah gets praise from the writer of Hebrews: "By faith Noah, being warned by God concerning events as yet unseen, in reverent fear constructed an ark for the saving of his household. By this he condemned the world and became an heir of the righteousness that comes by faith" (Hebrews 11:7). It all starts with Noah's faith. The faith came first. Without faith that God was who He said He was and the concomitant trust that He would send the flood like He said He would, there wouldn't be much reason for Noah to obey nor to act righteously. As the Hebrews passage tells us, "Without faith it is impossible to please him, for whoever would draw near to God must believe that he exists and that he rewards those who seek him" (Hebrews 11:6). Pleasing God is being obedient. Without faith, true obedience will not happen.

Can you obey Jesus if you don't know Him? I don't think so. Obeying is an interpersonal thing. You need to acknowledge someone else's authority over you before you can obey. It is true that some unbelievers act in ways that, for example, are in accord with the Ten Commandments. But if someone has not given their life to Christ, then they are not obeying Christ. Their actions, which may be in accord with the Ten Commandments, have other motivations. They are obeying themselves for their own glory, or another god, or an unknown god. These may be who Jesus is talking about in Matthew 7:23 when He says, "I never knew you; depart from me, you workers of lawlessness."

With faith, true obedience to God can happen. But it does not necessarily happen. Noah needed to choose to obey. And he did choose to obey, and thereby remained in a walk with God. And when you walk with God, you act in godly ways. That made Noah righteous and blameless.

And it wasn't just in building the ark that Noah obeyed God. Noah obeyed God throughout the entire flood journey. Repeatedly in the text we see that Noah did all that the Lord commanded him. Noah walked with God every step of the way. This is what it means to be righteous: to surrender completely to God's commands. And when we do, God can use us to accomplish His work of salvation, just as God used Noah to save the human race.

When we have faith, it allows us to walk with God. When we then obey, we continue to walk with Him. As we continue to walk with Him, we go along the paths in which He leads us, which allows God to use us for His purposes and ultimately for His glory.

Other Lessons from the Rising Action

As the rising action continues, the ark travels safely through the devastation as the outside world is annihilated. This is clearly a preview of sorts of the second coming, when Jesus will return and judge the world. At that time the ungodly will be "slain by the sword that came from the mouth of him who was sitting on the horse, and all the birds" will be gorged with their flesh (Revelation 19:21). Just as humanity was wiped out during the flood, so the ungodly will be wiped out on the Day of the Lord, and only those of faith will be spared. As we will see later, Jesus and Peter used the flood story in this figurative way, as a tool for teaching about the second coming. In a related manner, the flood also provides a figure of salvation. Just as God spared Noah from the flood, He will spare His own from the coming judgment on the Day of the Lord. Bruce Waltke puts it well when he writes, "The elect covenant family going through a sea of death and coming forth from their burial chamber is a pledge that the redeemed will be brought through the cataclysm of the final judgment."[230]

The ark can also operate as a figure of the kingdom of God. In this metaphor, the members of the kingdom of God are set apart from the unbelievers and from the entire world system. And we are set apart via

God's grace, just as in the flood story God shut Noah and his family into the ark (Genesis 7:16). The kingdom travels through the world like the ark travels through the water. Members of the kingdom are in the world but not a part of the world. Our journey is difficult, and we get tossed around by the waves of life, but we are protected from the spiritual death outside in the world. As Jesus says, "I give them eternal life, and they will never perish, and no one will snatch them out of my hand" (John 10:28). Eventually, we will pass the trials of this life, disembark from the ark, and inhabit a new world. The apostle John saw a vision of "a new heaven and a new earth, for the first heaven and the first earth had passed away, and the sea was no more" (Revelation 21:1). Having been preserved in the ark for eternal life, we will enter the new Jerusalem, prepared for us "as a bride adorned for her husband" (Revelation 21:2).

Notes

230   Bruce K. Waltke, *Genesis* (Grand Rapids, MI: Zondervan Academic, 2001), 152.

CHAPTER 28

....

Climax, Falling Action, and Resolution

The Climax

The climax of the flood story, in the pattern of Freytag's Pyramid, is the single sentence at 8:1a: "But God remembered Noah and all the beasts and all the livestock that were with him in the ark." This is also a reversal in the tradition of Aristotle's poetics. In reality, God had never forgotten Noah. He was preserving Noah all the while, and for Noah's sake God reversed the flood in 8:1b. Another way to look at it is that, for God, remembering is relational, not mental.[231] Here at the climax, the author emphasizes the reversal in approach that God takes to His problem—the problem of being separated from humanity by humanity's sin. Instead of wiping us out and starting over, God spares humanity and will offer a new way to reunite with us, via Jesus.

A few points are worth lingering on for a moment. First, God keeps His promises. He is trustworthy. Second, God protects His own. God protected Noah from the largest imaginable catastrophe. Believers, of course, suffer hardship and disease and death like everyone else, but God protects us from the raging floodwaters of the spiritual realm. Satan cannot steal us from the bosom of Christ. The third point, related to the second, is that the righteous will survive the coming judgment of the world. Due to Noah's faith and obedience, he survived the flood. Indeed, more than mere survival, Noah was blessed. The flood story prefigures the end of the world. At Jesus's second coming He will remember His own. As believers, we will be vindicated, spared from judgment and placed in a new creation.

The Falling Action

This theme of new creation is prominent in the falling action of the story, which begins in 8:1b and continues through 8:19. It begins with God making a wind blow over the earth, causing the waters to subside. The key point of 8:1b, and really of the entire falling action segment, is that God is recreating the earth. The author makes sure we get this point by using language that echoes the creation account. In Genesis 1:2, the Spirit of God, which can also be translated as the "wind of God," was hovering over the waters. Here, a wind blows over the earth. Next, the windows of the firmament are closed, and the water recedes, such that the waters above the firmament are again separated from the waters below the firmament as in day two of creation. The tops of the mountains soon appear, similar to the land being created in day three. Eventually, animals and humans return to the earth as in day six. The story ends with God blessing humanity in chapter 9, using similar language as in Genesis 1.

When Noah steps off the ark, he is stepping into a re-creation, a new creation. The old earth has been wiped out; God has started over. Noah, as many commentators have stressed, is a new Adam. The old Adam failed and was cast from the garden. Noah grows his own garden but sins in it. And thus the world begins to disobey God once more. The world needed a true new Adam, someone who would

CLIMAX, FALLING ACTION, AND RESOLUTION

be perfectly obedient and forever connected to the Tree of Life—and who could offer us access as well. For such a person, humanity had to wait for Jesus.

The falling action contains another lesson that I find interesting. Noah alone was righteous, yet his sons and their wives were saved as well. They ventured onto the ark and survived. I think Chris Hodges explains this situation well. We all have a sphere of influence, and if we act righteously, that can rub off on those closest to us.[232] As Hodges discusses, Acts 16:31 touches on the same point. In this passage, God has just busted Paul and Silas out of prison, and the jailer has asked Paul and Silas what he must do to be saved. They respond, "Believe in the Lord Jesus, and you will be saved, you and your household." The meaning of the word "household" may be rendered as not only an immediate family, but all whom the jailer had responsibility for or a close relationship with. The Bible seems to be emphasizing that we all need to take our role as spiritual leaders seriously. I strongly suspect that most of us were helped on our way toward Christ by the words, examples, prayers, and encouragements of Christians, whether they were family members, friends, pastors, or people God providentially put into our lives at the right moments.

The Resolution

The resolution to the flood story is given in 9:1–17 and starts with a blessing. God's wrath has been satisfied, and He wills humanity to flourish. God promises not to destroy the whole world with another flood. Humanity will continue on despite its wickedness. This teaches us about God's grace, but in more ways than may be obvious. Yes, God was indeed graceful toward the people in Noah's day, giving them 120 years to repent before bringing judgment. And God indeed showed grace to Noah, although this should not be pushed too far. God spared Noah's life, yes, but God could have simply taken him up to heaven like God did with Enoch, who like Noah "walked with God" (Genesis 5:22, 6:9). Instead, God had Noah endure a brutal and harrowing year-long voyage and then dumped him out onto a blighted landscape. So while God did show grace to Noah and his family and the people of that day, I initially found it awkward to talk of God's grace in the midst of a story in which God kills virtually everyone and everything on the planet. Until I realized that in this story, God's grace is mainly extended to *us*. When God spared the world, He spared us, who never would have been born had God abandoned His project altogether. Man's heart is still evil (see again Genesis 8:21), and God is still a God of holiness and judgment, so God should have taken Noah up and let humanity perish. Think about it from God's point of view: The ultimate purpose of this world is to give people an opportunity to join Him in the afterlife. But since we are wicked and, as a result, couldn't stand in God's presence for even a moment, never mind eternity, there was no point in keeping the world. But rather than scrap the world, God decided to salvage it. He provided a way—Jesus—for us to be washed clean and be with Him. This world has a cosmic purpose.

God's grace to us reveals His love for us. The deeper our depravity, the greater the love required for Him to redeem us. No matter how sinful we are, God's love is greater. And humanity's depravity is such that it justifies the destruction of the world. The height of God's love is correspondingly immense. As every intention and every thought within our hearts is perpetually evil (Genesis 6:5), so the steadfast intention of God's heart is to love. God's love for us is permanent, perfect, infinite, and eternal. Motivated by this great love, God chose to pay the price for our rebellion Himself. All the punishment that we as believers deserve, the Father inflicted upon Jesus at the cross. Thus Jesus says in John 3:16, "For God so loved the world, that he gave his only Son, that whoever believes in him should not perish but have eternal life." As D. A. Carson says about this verse, "God's love is to be admired because the world is so bad, and God's love is a testimony to His character."[233] And this love that He has for each of us is indeed eternal. Through the ark, God loved each one of us, even though we had not been born yet. God is outside of space and time and has loved us since before the beginning of time. As Paul writes in Ephesians 1:4–5, God "chose us in him before the foundation of the world, that we should be holy and blameless before him. In love he predestined us for adoption to himself as sons through Jesus Christ, according to the purpose of his will."

Notes

231 Paul Copan and Douglas Jacoby, *Origins* (Nashville: Morgan James, 2019), 167.

232 Chris Hodges, "Noah," sermon at Church of the Highlands, February 12, 2012, https://www.churchofthehighlands.com/media/message/noah.

233 D. A. Carson, *The Gospel According to John*, The Pillar New Testament Commentary (Grand Rapids, MI: Eerdmans, 1991), 205.

CHAPTER 29

Consistency with Other Bible Passages

At this point in my journey I felt very comfortable with my understanding of the Genesis flood story with regard to its significant figurative elements, its relation to ancient Near Eastern literature, and its interpretative meanings. I was still worried, however, because I needed to make sure all of this squared with the other passages in the Bible that concern the flood. The New Testament passages, in particular those from 1 and 2 Peter, were a real challenge for me and caused me much angst. As I mentioned, these passages seem to be talking about a global flood, and on a surface level seem to affirm a global flood. It was hard as well to find helpful resources. As far as I could find, few people seemed to talk, write, or blog about these passages in relation to the historicity of the Noah story, except for YEC commentators, who argue that they affirm a literal interpretation.

Eventually, persistence paid off. The key concept that unlocked the puzzle is this: Just as the Genesis story has significant figurative elements, the biblical authors used the flood story in a figurative sense. They were not affirming the historical interpretation against a figurative interpretation. They were not concerned with the distinction at all. Instead, they were using the flood story, which tells of a figurative global flood, in order to make theological points. Referencing a story with figurative elements does not turn it into a factual narrative. Indeed, Longman and Walton argue that the New Testament authors (and Jesus Himself) were sophisticated enough to understand that the Genesis story was a figurative telling—a large local flood portrayed as a global event so that it could teach theological lessons.[234]

I am not as confident as Longman and Walton seem to be that the biblical authors did not believe in a literal global flood. Regardless, they used the flood figuratively in their inspired writings, and it is the lessons from the flood that became inspired truth. To again cite Longman and Walton, "The New Testament writers have no independent access to the event. Their inspiration does not grant them insider information, only authoritative interpretation of the meaning of the flood event and its application."[235] The authors could have had incorrect scientific and historical beliefs on the flood while maintaining perfect theological insight.

Let's take the flood-related passages one by one and investigate, placing extra attention on the passages from 1 and 2 Peter as they are, in my opinion, more challenging to interpret.

Noah in the Old Testament

The first appearance by Noah after Genesis is 1 Chronicles 1:4, where he is simply listed in a genealogy. The next Old Testament passage is Isaiah 54:9, which reads, "This is like the days of Noah to me: as I swore that the waters of Noah should no more go over the earth, so I have sworn that I will not be angry with you, and will not rebuke you." For context, it is useful to go back to the previous chapter, Isaiah 53. In that famous chapter, God foretells of Jesus's suffering and sacrificial death. Here in Isaiah 54, the Lord speaks of the result of that sacrifice: an everlasting covenant of peace between God and those who trust in

Jesus, the members of the kingdom of heaven. In verse 9 above, God (speaking through His prophet Isaiah) uses an analogy to explain His covenant. The new "covenant of peace" (Isaiah 54:10) with believers is compared to the covenant that God made with Noah after the flood. Just as God then promised never again to destroy the world, God now promises that His "steadfast love shall not depart" (Isaiah 54:10) from believers. The important thing to recognize is that the analogy holds whether the first leg is regarded as a literal global flood or as a hyperbolic portrayal of a local flood. The crux is that the covenant in Genesis 9 covered all of humanity. From a slightly different angle, we can say that whether the account of Genesis 6–9 is literal or figurative, it is truth nonetheless. And as it is truth, it can be used as the first leg of an analogy. So Isaiah 54:9 sheds no additional light on whether we ought to interpret the flood story as literal or figurative. The prophecy simply repeats some of the key details found in the Genesis account.

The last Old Testament passage to reference Noah occurs in Ezekiel (14:14, 20). Verse 14 states that "even if these three men, Noah, Daniel, and Job, were in it, they would deliver but their own lives by their righteousness." The "it" here refers to the land of Israel. In the broader passage, the Lord is angry at Israel for their widespread worship of idols. God declares that Israel will not be spared punishment for this offense. Noah was, like Job and Daniel, a man of remarkable faith and righteousness. Yet this offense against God was such that if a man with Noah's level of faith and righteousness existed in Israel at that time, that man's faith and righteousness would serve to spare merely himself. That man would not be able to save even his family (from exile). God is here emphasizing the extent and depth of Israel's sin. The passage does not bear on the flood and does not teach about the extent of the flood. The mention of Noah in verse 20 serves the same purpose and does not need to be treated separately.

Noah in the New Testament

The first mention of Noah or the flood in the New Testament is found in Matthew 24:36–39:

> *³⁶But concerning that day and hour no one knows, not even the angels of heaven, nor the Son, but the Father only. ³⁷For as were the days of Noah, so will be the coming of the Son of Man. ³⁸For as in those days before the flood they were eating and drinking, marrying and giving in marriage, until the day when Noah entered the ark, ³⁹and they were unaware until the flood came and swept them all away, so will be the coming of the Son of Man.*

Christ is talking here about His second coming. The point is that we do not know when that day will come, and its arrival will come as a surprise to most. The lesson is that we should not be so preoccupied with the details of our daily lives that we leave ourselves unprepared to greet Christ. We must stay awake (verse 42) and be ready (verse 44), obeying God by doing His will (verses 45–46). The meaning of this passage, then, concerns the second coming and not the flood. The story of the flood is used as an instrument to convey the inspired truth about the second coming. Note well that the example of the flood, in this context, is useful whether Genesis depicts a literal global flood or provides a figurative portrayal, and whether the flood was a global deluge or a large local flood.

Noah is next mentioned in Luke's genealogy of Jesus: "the son of Cainan, the son of Arphaxad, the son of Shem, the son of Noah, the son of Lamech" (Luke 3:36). This shows that Noah was in the line of Jesus. This verse provides an argument for the historicity of Noah but does not make any claims about the flood.

Luke 17:26–27 also mention Noah, but it is a parallel passage to Matthew 24:36–39, so we do not need to treat it separately.

Noah makes an appearance in the "Hall of Fame of Faith" of Hebrews 11: "By faith Noah, being warned by God concerning events as yet unseen, in reverent fear constructed an ark for the saving of his household. By this he condemned the world and became an heir of the righteousness that comes by faith" (Hebrews 11:7). For context, note that in Hebrews 10, the author encourages believers to "draw near with a true heart in full assurance of faith" (Hebrews 10:22) and to be among "those who have faith and preserve their souls" (Hebrews 10:39). Hebrews 11 begins with a definition of faith as "the assurance of things hoped for, the conviction of things not seen" (Hebrews 11:1). The chapter then tours the book of Genesis, highlighting men and women who are exemplars of faith. Noah, of course, is included in this list. And how perfectly does Noah fit the definition! By building the ark in anticipation of the flood, Noah displayed a conviction that the flood would indeed come. The teaching of the passage is clearly about Noah's faith, not the flood. The author uses the flood story incidentally to show Noah's faith. As such, the author is not teaching on the scope of the flood. Again, the author is content to frame the story as it is presented in Genesis. It is also worth noting that the use of the word "world" in Hebrews 11:7 does not show that the flood was global. Through Noah's faith in building the ark, and through the flood itself, the world and the entire world system were judged to be guilty, but this does not necessarily indicate a global flood. The verse says that the world was condemned and found guilty, not flooded.

1 Peter 3:20

Now we get to the difficult passages in 1 Peter and 2 Peter. I should note here that there is some amount of controversy over whether the apostle Peter wrote these letters or whether they were instead written by an unknown author using this pseudonym. I do not wish to weigh in on that controversy. For simplicity, I'll refer to the author as being the apostle, but the inspired meaning of the texts does not change either way.

The next appearance of Noah in the New Testament is in 1 Peter 3:20. This is in the middle of a notoriously difficult passage, one of the most difficult in the New Testament. As context, Peter is writing a letter to encourage Christians who are being persecuted for their faith. Just before our passage, Peter stresses that the audience should persevere in their faith and maintain good and holy behavior even while being persecuted. The passage we'll look at is 3:18–22.

> [18]*For Christ also suffered once for sins, the righteous for the unrighteous, that he may bring us to God, being put to death in the flesh but made alive in the spirit,* [19]*in which he went and proclaimed to the spirits in prison,* [20]*because they formerly did not obey, when God's patience waited in the days of Noah, while the ark was being prepared, in which a few, that is, eight persons, were brought safely through water.* [21]*Baptism, which corresponds to this, now saves you, not as a removal of dirt from the body but as an appeal to God for a good conscience, through the resurrection of Jesus Christ,* [22]*who has gone into heaven and is at the right hand of God, with angels, authorities, and powers having been subjected to him.*

The main thrust of the passage is that Jesus suffered for doing good, and in order to do good; as a result, He is glorified in heaven, where He rules over all at the right hand of the Father. In a similar way, we should persevere through persecution in obedience to God and with hope in Christ, for we will be delivered to glory as well because of our salvation in the cross. Peter uses the story of the flood to drive home this point, comparing the audience with Noah and his family and binding the analogy further with the symbolic use of water.

Let's start our analysis of this passage on the outside, then move to the middle. In verse 18, Peter offers Jesus as the exemplar of suffering for doing good, stressing that He suffered and died unjustly but was raised from the dead (made alive in the spirit). After being raised, Jesus went into heaven, where He has authority (verse 22) even over angels and all heavenly beings, including all those who disobey (demons). When we suffer persecution, we should use Jesus as a model, persevering on earth and looking forward to our eternal reward. As Thomas Schreiner writes, "Even though Jesus suffered death in terms of his body, the Spirit raised him from the dead. Similarly, those who belong to Christ, even though they will face suffering, will ultimately share in Christ's resurrection."[236]

Verse 19 shows the cleverness of Peter's writing, as he refers to "spirits in prison" both to set up Christ's glory in verse 22 and to introduce the Noah comparison in verse 20. Modern scholarship has coalesced around the interpretation of "spirits in prison" as being fallen angels, and verse 19 referring "to Christ's victory proclamation following his resurrection as he ascended to take his rightful place in heaven as the ruler over all."[237, 238] Jesus proclaims His victory to all fallen angels, and emblematic of these are those who disobeyed in the time before the flood, which we discussed above in connection with Genesis 6:1–4. Whether angels did or did not cohabit with humans prior to the flood, Peter's audience may have thought that they did, based upon the non-canonical book of 1 Enoch. At any rate, there were doubtlessly demons around before the flood, whether or not they engaged in that particular sin. The point is that Jesus is victorious over all, even fallen angels.

Peter now moves the action to the flood. Peter's audience could identify with Noah. Noah and his family were but a small number of people; they were surrounded by unbelievers and mocked for their faith. In Asia Minor (modern-day Turkey), where Peter's letter circulated, the comparatively few Christians of the region were being mocked and persecuted for their faith. Even though Noah and his family were few, the Lord rescued them, leading them through the cataclysm via the ark. Noah and his family emerged into a new creation, with a rainbow signifying God's covenant with them. In a similar way, Peter's audience was urged to persevere through their suffering in the days before the second coming, with the rightful expectation that God would shepherd them through their tribulations and bless them on the far side with eternal fellowship.

Peter next ties the analogy tighter through the symbolic use of water. He compares the flood waters to the waters of baptism. Just as Noah's survival through the flood waters revealed his faith and righteousness and placed him in a new creation, the readers' emergence from the waters of baptism reveal their coming salvation and the rewards for their righteousness. Peter may have been drawing on Babylonian traditions here. In ancient Babylon, most people couldn't swim. Throwing someone in a river was a common way to test someone's innocence or guilt regarding a crime. If they survived this trial by water, it was conceived that they were innocent, and thus they were vindicated.[239]

Peter is making the point that the readers' trials are like the flood. In the flood, Noah's faith and righteousness were proved by his safe passage. In the same way, a believer's baptism reveals their decision to accept the salvation offered to them by the resurrection. As Schreiner puts it, "Submersion under the water represents death. ... Believers survive the death-dealing baptismal waters because they are baptized with Christ. They are rescued from death through his resurrection."[240] Likewise Charles Spurgeon wrote, "The ark and immersion set forth the same truth. The man is 'buried in baptism,' to signify that he is dead to the world; wherein also he rises again to show his fellowship with Christ in resurrection, and the fact that he has risen to newness of life. Baptism is a picture of the way of salvation, just as Noah's ark was."[241]

During a typical evangelical baptism, the pastor says the phrase "buried in the likeness of His death" as he submerges the Christian in the water, and "raised in the likeness of His resurrection" as he removes the Christian from the water. Likewise, "Peter's readers will be among those who escape the second 'flood' of judgment because they have already passed through the waters of Christian baptism, which saves them by virtue of the vindicating resurrection of Jesus Christ."[242]

Now that we understand the context and message of the passage, we can address the question that here concerns us: Is the reference to eight survivors in verse 20 an inspired statement that the flood was literally global? The answer is no. We have seen in our explanation of the passage that Peter uses the flood as an archetypal event and as part of an analogy. As Karen Jobes relates, "He uses the flood as a type of God's catastrophic judgment, which happened only after God's restrained patience, and he poses the survival of Noah from that divine judgment as a type of Christian salvation, which involves the tamed waters of baptism."[243] The Holy Spirit is not using this text to teach about whether the flood account in Genesis was literal or figurative. God is teaching us about how and why to suffer through persecution. In the passage, Peter makes figurative use of the flood story, comparing it to the readers' circumstances. With regard to the number of survivors, Peter mentions this number to make the point that although the readers' numbers were few relative to the numbers of their persecutors, God would save them. Peter uses the flood story in a figurative sense, not in a literal sense. He uses it theologically, not scientifically. The details of the flood story are being used incidentally to further the message of how and why Christians should endure persecution.

2 Peter 2:5

Next up is 2 Peter 2:1–10a. This letter was written to the same churches as 1 Peter, but the context is different. In 2 Peter, Peter is warning the churches about false teachers who deny the second coming; their behavior is characterized by deep and pervasive sin, and they will be judged by God:

¹But false prophets also arose among the people, just as there will be false teachers among you, who will secretly bring in destructive heresies, even denying the Master who bought them, bringing upon themselves swift destruction. ²And many will follow their sensuality, and because of them the way of truth will be blasphemed. ³And in their greed they will exploit you with false words. Their condemnation from long ago is not idle, and their destruction is not asleep.

⁴For if God did not spare angels when they sinned, but cast them into hell and committed them to chains of gloomy darkness to be kept until the judgment; ⁵if he did not spare the ancient world, but preserved Noah, a herald of righteousness, with seven others, when he brought a flood upon the world of the ungodly; ⁶if by turning the cities of Sodom and Gomorrah to ashes he condemned them to extinction, making them an example of what is going to happen to the ungodly; ⁷and if he rescued righteous Lot, greatly distressed by the sensual conduct of the wicked ⁸(for as that righteous man lived among them day after day, he was tormenting his righteous soul over their lawless deeds that he saw and heard); ⁹then the Lord knows how to rescue the godly from trials, and to keep the unrighteous under punishment until the day of judgment, ¹⁰and especially those who indulge in the lust of defiling passion and despise authority.

What Peter is teaching here is that God judges sin, and thus He will judge the false teachers. In verse 1 we see that "false prophets deny the sovereign lordship of Jesus Christ."²⁴⁴ Such teachers claim to be Christians but are hypocrites, and will be judged. In verse 2, we see that the false teachers refuse to live godly lives, instead following after the lusts of the flesh. Later in the chapter Peter calls them "slaves of corruption" (verse 19). So we have sinful teachers who do not recognize Jesus as Lord and who are leading others astray. As John

MacArthur notes, "Nothing is more wicked than for someone to claim to speak for God to the salvation of souls when in reality he speaks for Satan to the damnation of souls."[245] Peter points out in verse 3 that the Old Testament teaches us how God deals with sin. He does not mess around.

Then, starting in verse 4, Peter goes back into the Old Testament and picks out three such examples of how God judges sin. In keeping with an important theme of salvation that he continues to develop later in the letter and to provide encouragement to his readers, two of Peter's three examples also involve the rescue of the righteous. One of those two examples is God's rescue of Lot, his wife, and Lot's two daughters from the destruction of Sodom and Gomorrah (although Lot's wife didn't quite make it out alive due to her disobedience, as we discussed earlier). The other encouraging example Peter employs is that of the great flood, wherein God destroyed the entire world but saved righteous Noah and his seven family members. The pinnacle of the passage is verse 9. God will rescue the godly and will punish the unrighteous false teachers.

Peter is using the truth provided in the Old Testament to teach the audience a lesson about their current circumstances. Were those particular Old Testament passages meant to be interpreted literally or figuratively? Or were they literal accounts with figurative elements? No matter the answer, the underlying fact is that these passages are filled with truth that is good for teaching. All biblical teaching, whether expressed in literal or figurative vehicles, is God's truth. Thus Peter's reference to the universality of the flood, and in particular the mention of eight survivors, is not evidence that the flood story is a literal account. Rather, Peter is using the story as presented, figurative elements and all, to make his theological point. Just like the ungodly were judged in the flood, the false teachers will be judged at the second coming. Meanwhile, the readers will be vindicated at the second coming, as Noah was vindicated by the flood.

2 Peter 3:6

The last New Testament verse we will discuss is 2 Peter 3:6. Here is the broader passage, 2 Peter 3:3–10:

> *3:3knowing this first of all, that scoffers will come in the last days with scoffing, following their own sinful desires. 4They will say, "Where is the promise of his coming? For ever since the fathers fell asleep, all things are continuing as they were from the beginning of creation." 5For they deliberately overlook this fact, that the heavens existed long ago, and the earth was formed out of water and through water by the word of God, 6and that by means of these the world that then existed was deluged with water and perished. 7But by the same word the heavens and earth that now exist are stored up for fire, being kept until the day of judgment and destruction of the ungodly.*
>
> *8But do not overlook this one fact, beloved, that with the Lord one day is as a thousand years, and a thousand years as one day. 9The Lord is not slow to fulfill his promise as some count slowness, but is patient toward you, not wishing that any should perish, but that all should reach repentance. 10But the day of the Lord will come like a thief, and then the heavens will pass away with a roar, and the heavenly bodies will be burned up and dissolved, and the earth and the works that are done on it will be exposed.*

The context of this passage is that false teachers, whom Peter refers to as scoffers, would arise who would deny the second coming of Christ. Many members of the early church expected Jesus to return soon, even within their lifetimes. They were thus sensitive to taunts such as "Where is the promise of his coming?" Or, rendered rhetorically, "Where is Jesus? Shouldn't He have come (again) by now?" The scoffers taunted the church to rob believers' hope and to argue that they themselves, the scoffers, would escape judgment for their sinful lifestyles—the lifestyles Peter discusses at length in the preceding chapter and alludes to in verse 3.

As justification for their taunt, the scoffers point out that since the fathers fell asleep, all things are continuing as normal. There is debate as to who "the fathers" are. The term is used elsewhere to mean the Old Testament patriarchs. Many, however, including Richard Bauckham,[246] think that "the fathers" refers to the first generation of Christians. This latter interpretation makes sense in the context of the passage, as the scoffers would be saying, "Jesus was supposed to come back in your lifetimes. Well, you have been dying off due to age and martyrdom, and that whole end-of-the-world thing hasn't begun yet."

Anyway, regardless of the interpretation of "the fathers," it seems clear that the scoffers are saying that the fact that Jesus hasn't yet returned is evidence that He isn't going to come at all. This is the argument that Peter addresses in the rest of the passage. Peter responds to this argument by going straight to Scripture, showing that Jesus has the means and the motive to return and judge the world; He is merely waiting for the proper opportunity. In verse 5, Peter refers back to Genesis 1 and the creation of the heavens and the earth, and especially days two and three, which feature the role of water and the separation of water in the acts of creation. His point is that God (Jesus, in fact) created the world by His Word, so He can surely destroy it. Jesus has the means. In verse 6, Peter uses the symbolism of water in creation and in the flood story to transition from creation to judgment. As the Genesis flood story reveals, God judges sin. And so it makes sense that Jesus will, at the appropriate time, destroy the world. Jesus has motive. In verse 7, Peter explains that since God has the means and the motive to destroy the world, it is just a matter of waiting for the appropriate opportunity, the appropriate time, to do so. Peter uses the image of fire to evoke Old Testament prophecies of the second coming: "For behold, the LORD will come in fire, and his chariots like the whirlwind, to render his anger in fury, and his rebuke with flames of fire. For by fire will the LORD enter into judgment" (Isaiah 66:15–16a).

In verse 8, Peter refers back to Psalm 90:4: "For a thousand years in your sight are but as yesterday when it is past, or as a watch in the night." Contrary to what Peter's readers may have believed, this proper time would not necessarily come in their lifetimes. In verse 9, he gives the reason for the seeming delay: God is patient and wishes many to be saved. We see this sentiment expressed throughout the Bible. "Therefore the LORD waits to be gracious to you, and therefore he exalts himself to show mercy to you" (Isaiah 30:18); "For I have no pleasure in the death of anyone, declares the Lord God; so turn, and live" (Ezekiel 18:32). Peter closes in verse 10 by stating that when the means and motive are met by the right timing—the proper opportunity—Jesus will come unexpectedly and with might. Peter refers to words Jesus Himself spoke: "But know this, that if the master of the house had known in what part of the night the thief was coming, he would have stayed awake and would not have let his house be broken into" (Matthew 24:43).

Peter also alludes to the several Old Testament verses that foretell of the destruction at the second coming. One such verse is Micah 1:4. First, note that the NKJV translation of 2 Peter 3:10 reads, "But the day of the Lord will come as a thief in the night, in which the heavens will pass away with a great noise, and the elements will melt with fervent heat; both the earth and the works that are in it will be burned up." Now read Micah 1:4—"And the mountains will melt under him, and the valleys will split open, like wax before the fire, like waters poured down a steep place"—and note the references to melting in each verse.

The scoffers lacked true faith, and that lack of faith was the poison that produced such vile fruit. Because of that lack of faith, they did not trust in the Word of the Lord. The Word created the world (verse 5), sustains the world (verse 7), and laid out in Scripture the very step-by-step argument that Peter uses to refute them.

The role of the flood in Peter's argument is to demonstrate that Jesus has motive to judge the world—He judges sin. As we saw earlier, the Holy Spirit used figurative elements in the flood story to clearly reveal this truth in Genesis. Peter is using the flood story as it is presented in Genesis to affirm the truth that is provided there. He is neither relying on the flood account being literal nor teaching that it is literal.

Notes

234   Tremper Longman III and John H. Walton, *The Lost World of the Flood* (Downers Grove, IL: IVP Academic, 2018), 99.

235   Longman and Walton, 96.

236   Thomas R. Schreiner, *1, 2 Peter, Jude*, The New American Commentary (Nashville: B&H, 2003), 184.

237   Karen H. Jobes, *1 Peter*, Baker Exegetical Commentary of the New Testament (Grand Rapids, MI: Baker Academic, 2005), 237.

238   Other interpretations include Jesus preaching through the mouth of Noah in the days before the flood, and Jesus descending into hell to preach to the fallen angels and/or humans who died before the time of Christ.

239   Tremper Longman III, *Genesis*, The Story of God Bible Commentary, eds. Tremper Longman III and Scot McKnight (Grand Rapids, MI: Zondervan, 2016), 122.

240   Schreiner, *1, 2 Peter, Jude*, 194.

241   Charles Haddon Spurgeon, "Shut in or Shut Out," The Spurgeon Center for Biblical Preaching at Midwestern Seminary, accessed September 20, 2019, https://www.spurgeon.org/resource-library/sermons/shut-in-or-shut-out#flipbook.

242   Karen H. Jobes, *1 Peter*, Baker Exegetical Commentary of the New Testament (Grand Rapids, MI: Baker Academic, 2005), 252.

243   Jobes, 247.

244   John MacArthur, *The MacArthur Study Bible* (Wheaton, IL: Crossway, 2010), 1905.

245   MacArthur, 1904.

246   Richard Bauckham, *Jude–2 Peter*, World Biblical Commentary (Grand Rapids, MI: Zondervan, 1983), 290–91.

CHAPTER 30

A Way Forward

If you agree with the case I've laid out for a figurative understanding of the creation and flood accounts, what do we do with our new knowledge and understanding? Do we go out and try to convince our YEC friends of our positions? I think we should be careful and sensitive about that. Trying to "convert" YEC friends who are secure in their faith and confident in their views on the flood and creation may be ill-advised. Especially if pushing them toward a new way of thinking could be disruptive to their Christian walk. Many Christians are firmly wedded to a literal interpretation. If they are thriving in their Christian walk with their literal interpretation, it may be best not to rock that boat.

Something we should stress with our YEC brethren, however, is that early Genesis is something Christians can agree to disagree on. The literal interpretation is not the only valid one. Many Christians hold to old earth interpretations of early Genesis. Many others and I believe figurative interpretations as laid out in this book offer the most fruitful avenue for understanding early Genesis. This is okay. We are not disagreeing about the empty tomb. We are acknowledging that there are different opinions about a section of Scripture that is particularly difficult to comprehend. We don't need to fight over this.

Acknowledging that there are different ways for a member of the body of Christ to interpret early Genesis will allow us to minister to our brethren for whom literal interpretations are not satisfying. When a brother or sister who does not accept YEC claims is tempted to doubt God's Word or is striving and struggling to understand Scripture, we can and should point them to figurative interpretations as laid out in this book and in the books and other resources that I have referenced.

And when we are faced with questions, doubts, or criticisms from unbelievers who discount the historicity of the creation and flood accounts, it may be productive to turn to figurative means of interpreting the text. Doing so will aid us in defending the Bible and may make it easier for some hearts to turn to Christ.

The above discussion focuses on adults. But what should we teach children? Parenting around the flood in particular can be difficult, and I'll focus on that here, although the same things can be said regarding creation. In Sunday school and at home with their children's Bibles, kids are often taught to view the flood story from a literal perspective. And that makes sense to me. Little kids don't understand figurative language, and anyway they would not appreciate the connections with *Atrahasis* and the like. Besides, a literal reading of the flood story presents many valuable lessons for children.

It could be argued that the best approach is to run this forward until the kids are adults, teaching them from a literal interpretation straight through until they are 18. After all, maybe they will remain comfortable with a literal interpretation their whole lives, so why rock the boat by introducing figurative perspectives? Or if they do come to doubt the literal interpretation, perhaps they will resolve their doubts successfully on their own, one way or another; they may decide to stick with a belief in a literal global flood, take the OEC view, or perhaps adopt a figurative perspective.

In my personal opinion, I think it is often best to, at an appropriate age, let our children know that there are figurative interpretations that many Christians embrace. That way, if they ever come to have doubts about the literal account of the flood, they will know there are other interpretations to explore that they may become comfortable with. For high schoolers who express a desire to dig deeper into the text, I pray that the material in this book can be helpful. In this way, we can hopefully inoculate our kids against a science-based faith crisis that they might otherwise encounter in their late teens or beyond.

The challenge is picking the right age to introduce nonliteral interpretations. One problem is that, with kids, you often can't open the door just a crack. They will push it wide open. Here, that means that once you let them know that there are figurative interpretations, they may ask what those are. This would then naturally lead to discussions about potential figurative meanings of the early Genesis stories. The difficulty, again, is that young kids are not well suited for understanding figurative language. And further, even older kids may have trouble appreciating that some parts of Scripture are figurative and others are literal. The danger, then, is that exposing kids to figurative meanings too early could cause them to doubt the Bible.

I respect the tendency to shield kids from this potential pitfall. On the other hand, it may be best to prepare them for all the various ways in which people—both Christians and non-Christians—view early Genesis, and to do this before they run into an AronRa video. Or a college geology course. Our kids will unavoidably come across various views on early Genesis, including from atheists who assert that it has no truth content. They will also likely become exposed to scientific disciplines that dispute the historicity of the literal flood account. If our kids have by that time already started to think through, on their own, the interpretive challenges that early Genesis poses and have started to explore the depth, richness, and intricacy of the text from multiple points of view, they may be better able to withstand external challenges to their faith. It might be best to be proactive.

So what is an appropriate age? Every child is different, and every situation is different. I suspect it involves factors such as how well they can process figurative meaning, how inquisitive they are about different viewpoints on Scripture, how sheltered they are from non-Christian influences, how interested they are in science, and so on and so forth.

Of course, all that I've just written may sound nice, but then life hits you in the face. What do you do when you are put on the spot, and your child, who is still (too) young, asks you what you think about the flood? If you are like me, you fail, and then you ask Jesus to cover for your parenting mistakes. One day Clare, my oldest child, sat down next to me as I was doing research for this book. I must have been researching the flood because we started talking about it. She asked me if I believed in the flood. Now, this was a delicate moment. Clare was just beginning to get to know Jesus and hadn't yet given her life to Him. That would come a few months later, on Easter Sunday, 2019—praise the Lord! But at the time of this conversation, I sensed I should tread gingerly. Maybe I should have simply said yes (as I do believe there was a real flood, just not a global one), and otherwise put the conversation off. Maybe I should have simply encouraged her to look at the passage literally, and left it at that. Maybe I should have figured out an artful way to broach the topic of figurative meaning while still encouraging her to stick to a literal interpretation. Maybe I should have taken a roundabout approach, probing her ability to digest figurative meaning, and only continuing the conversation if I was comfortable with her responses. But instead I was blunt and just plainly told her that I thought that the flood happened, but that it didn't cover the entire world.

"So the Bible lied?!" Clare exclaimed. Panic surged inside me. I stammered something, trying to explain about figurative language, and I did a poor job of it. I went to full damage-control mode, simply and emphatically saying that no, the Bible did not lie at all, and the flood did occur (but I didn't say it was global). I think I contained the damage, and she didn't press me further at that time. What followed, on my end, was prayer.

It so happened that about five months after my disastrous conversation with Clare, she approached me again as I was just finishing a good rough draft of the flood portion of this book. She proceeded to again ask me if I believed in a global flood. Perhaps she was trying to open a conversation. I paused a moment. Clare was still 11, but closer to her 12th birthday than to her 11th. It had been almost half a year since our previous conversation on the issue. I sensed that she was better able to handle figurative meanings, and I knew her relationship with Jesus was stronger than it had been before. I was more circumspect this time but still rather artless. A mistake, again. But this time it turned out better. I stressed that many Christians disagree on the flood, and it is okay to disagree. From my perspective, I said, I didn't think there was a flood that covered the whole earth, but I trusted God's Word and just had a different viewpoint than many other Christians do on the scope of the event. "I don't think so either," she said. She quickly qualified herself. "Oh, I think there was a flood, but it wasn't everywhere." She added an explanation: "There were people living in Africa for the past, like, many, many years, and they weren't all killed by a flood." I was relieved. I would have been happy with whatever viewpoint she had, global flood or otherwise, so long as she wasn't doubting God because of the flood.

These conversations with Clare, and my journey throughout this book, brought home a lesson for me. The best thing we can do for our children with respect to this problem of the interpretation of early Genesis—and just flat-out the best thing we can do for them as parents, period—is to foster within them a love for Jesus and to encourage them to have their own personal relationship with Him. When storms come, there is no stronger mast to cling to than the Spirit of the living God inside you.

CPSIA information can be obtained
at www.ICGtesting.com
Printed in the USA
LVHW020313140920
665930LV00019B/665